Selected Poems

Anthony Hecht

Selected Poems

Edited by J. D. McClatchy

ALFRED A. KNOPF   *New York*   2017

THIS IS A BORZOI BOOK
PUBLISHED BY ALFRED A. KNOPF

The poems in this collection originally appeared in the following works:

A Summoning of Stones (MacMillan, 1954)
The Hard Hours (Atheneum, 1967)
Millions of Strange Shadows (Atheneum, 1977)
The Venetian Vespers (Atheneum, 1979)
The Transparent Man (Alfred A. Knopf, 1990)
Flight Among the Tombs (Alfred A. Knopf, 1996)
The Darkness and the Light (Alfred A. Knopf, 2001)

Library of Congress Cataloging-in-Publication Data
Hecht, Anthony, 1923–2004
[Poems. Selections]
Selected poems / by Anthony Hecht ; edited by J. D. McClatchy.
p.   cm.
ISBN 978-0-375-71198-5
I. McClatchy, J. D., 1945–   II. Title.
PS3558.E28A6 2011
811'.54—dc22   2010032374

Front cover photo by Michael Germana
Cover design by Carol Devine Carson

Manufactured in the United States of America
Published March 27, 2011
Reprinted Four Times
Sixth Printing, January 2017

Contents

Introduction

For every poet there are defining experiences: certain people and books, certain losses and sorrows, certain landscapes and themes that are compulsively revisited over the course of a career. One theorist would claim such experiences are unconscious, happen in one's earliest years, and haunt the writer ever after. A second theorist would insist there are inherent mythic patterns that shape a life, and the art made from that life. A third critic would contend that every writer struggles with his literary ancestors, desperately trying to overwrite them. Theories abound, and are always too narrow to contain the full scope of a poet's art. Still, any reader of Anthony Hecht's poems will sense that, for all their variety, they circle a few crucial preoccupations, and use their technical skill to speak about these in an especially charged and commanding manner.

An imaginary map of Hecht's sensibility would most certainly note how, as it were, Germany and Italy border each other. His experiences as a combatant in World War II and later as a sojourner in Italy were central for Hecht as landscapes over which deeper issues were deployed. When he deals with the Holocaust—as in "Rites and Ceremonies" or "Persistences" or "The Book of Yolek"—it is in a ritualistic or subdued manner that will allow him to address horrifying matters. And when he refers to his time in combat, it is usually a memory of utter isolation—far removed from the carnage and chaos, noise and camaraderie of actual warfare. In "Still Life," the poet is describing a lakeside just at dawn, and after talk of liquid leafage and glittering cobwebs, the poem pauses:

> Why does this so much stir me, like a code
>   Or muffled intimation
> Of purposes and preordained events?
> It knows me, and I recognize its mode

Of cautionary, spring-tight hesitation,
This silence so impacted and intense.

As in a water-surface I behold
    The first, soft, peach decree
Of light, its pale, inaudible commands.
I stand beneath a pine-tree in the cold,
Just before dawn, somewhere in Germany,
A cold, wet Garand rifle in my hands.

We know from other poems that this scene strangely duplicates scenes described from Hecht's childhood, where we find the lonely boy staring blankly out of the window, or standing paralyzed in front of a hill in winter. In other words, his wartime memories—of sickening fear or helplessness—serve to focus earlier, deeper memories, and the way they each recall and reinforce the other is part of the force of a Hecht poem. Even more telling is the contrast between such memories and the unexpected places they recur. In "A Hill," for instance, standing in a busy Italian piazza, the speaker is suddenly stricken with a memory of childhood. The extravagance of language used to describe the scene yields suddenly to a flat, stark speech. How often the gilded, luxuriant aspects of Italian landscape, architecture, or high art are lovingly rendered, only to be pulled like a sumptuous rug from under our feet. "My instinct for contrast and dialectic," he once explained to an interviewer, "is almost always at work, as a dramatic element of the poem, so that any flamboyance is likely to be confronted or opposed by counter-force directness, elemental grit." These counter-forces were at work throughout his career, and give his poems their dramatic momentum and fascination. Description and psychology pull against each other, finely observed textures can be suddenly ripped through like a stage backdrop. The diction in any one poem will veer giddily from high to low (in one poem, "Evangelist" is rhymed with "pissed").

"In each art," the poet Richard Wilbur has written, "the difficulty of the form is a substitute for the difficulty of direct apprehension and expression of the object." This accounts for the seeming contradiction between the subjects and shapes of many of Hecht's poems. Each of his books is stalked by occasions of madness, paranoia, hallucination, and dream; there are exile, plague, miscarriage, murder, genocide. Yet they are dramatized in stanzas of intricate construction and often grandiloquent diction. Form is meant as the long looking-glass, as a way of seeing the detail, the quaking heart, in the very midst of the muddle. He wants simultaneously to see the world and tell the truth. If Keats's urn is to be believed, and beauty is the whole truth, then the ravishingly beautiful stanzas of a Hecht poem—so intricately plotted, so lavishly detailed, their rhythms such that form and speech are a single pulse—would be truth enough. But a Hecht poem has always been something more. His is a *responsible* art, an art that responds to history, to political and domestic tragedies, with an awareness of personal accountability. The *beauty* of a Hecht poem, the very skill by which its material is revealed, often throws into an even stronger, more pathetic light the desolation of the human condition that is his subject. His poems are most moving when they offer their art to their subjects, when the poet finds words for the unspeakable, gives images and dramatic life to the inarticulate—a servant girl or battered child, a young woman dying of leukemia or a concentration-camp internee. The words and images he offers them, of course, enable the reader to share both the victim's forlorn aloneness and the poet's speculative freedom, both the baffled suffering of humankind and the consoling wonder of language.

The voice in Hecht's poems is like none other. Even so, he learned to speak in his very individual way by listening closely to earlier poets. Among his immediate forebears, two poets were crucial influences. One was T. S. Eliot, whose example helped shape not just Hecht's style but his sensibility, which, like Eliot's, is marked by a melancholy in the gloom of collapsed beliefs, occasionally startled by flashing glimpses of redemption. The other poet who helped Hecht toward his characteristic tone of voice was W. H. Auden, whose confidence in the mind's capacities resulted in a brilliant lexicon, a restless invention, an intellectual rigor, and an inclusive gaze. At the heart of both these poets' achievement is their way of confronting a loneliness of spirit that can be a curse or a blessing but is an inevitable concomitant of human life. Hecht's voice—whether we know it is a dramatic character's or presume it is his own—echoes that same loneliness: words piled against a vacancy, longing pitched against despair. Eliot and Auden were what we would call mid-Atlantic poets, straddling the two cultures, British and American. But both looked primarily to older English poets as muses, and Hecht did too. George Herbert, John Milton, and above all William Shakespeare were the poets he most admired, and each had a different distinction. Hecht liked Herbert's calm perfection of phrasing, Milton's architectonic rhetoric, and Shakespeare's breathtaking imagery and dramatic virtuosity. What all these poets share, of course, is the Biblical language that is the true heartbeat of traditional English poetry. In Hecht's work, the cadences and gravity of the King James Bible are everywhere. The dark visions of certain Old Testament books—Ecclesiastes, Isaiah, Jeremiah, Job—as well as the raptures of the Psalms and the narrative power of Matthew are intrinsic to his imagination.

To say that Anthony Hecht was a literary poet is only to claim for him what is important to every great poet. His style is a *composed* one, enriched by allusions to history and the literature of the past that he expects the reader to take notice of because they serve as an echo chamber within which his own poems' themes gather weight and resonance. In the same way, he often turned to traditional verse forms—sonnet, sestina, villanelle, and their kin—in part to pledge his allegiance to the continuity of English poetry. Any account of this aspect of his work, of course, implicates the far larger ambitions of the making and meanings of a poem. Hecht's "Peripeteia" memorably bows to this when a poem is described as "Governed by laws that stand for other laws, /

Both of which aim, through kindred disciplines, / At the soul's knowledge and habiliment." The rules of prosody, in other words, are moral principles meant finally to reveal the structure of human dilemmas and sympathies. Verse forms are one attempt at that. The sonnet's template or the villanelle's refrains are ways to shape the music of speech, and Hecht uses both received and invented forms as bracing structures inside which an argument unfolds. If the tone of his lines seems elevated, that is because all poetry is language heightened, and should sound out of the ordinary. If the texture seems complex, that is because he is acutely sensitive to the harmonies and dissonances of the line, to the syncopation of rhythms, to the way rhymes will manipulate and satisfy our expectations. "A serious and durable work of art, whatever its medium," he once wrote, "will make the sort of demands upon us that invite repeated experiences that will fail to exhaust the work." With each fresh reading, a Hecht poem reveals itself to be a prism, new facets mirroring new depths.

His books first appeared after long intervals but had an immediate authority. How did they change over the decades? *A Summoning of Stones* was published in 1954, when the poet was thirty-one years old. That his poems had been appearing in literary journals for seven years before the book came out is a sign of how fastidious he was about making a formal debut. He had long since sought out the teachers—John Crowe Ransom and Allen Tate—he thought would encourage the best in him, and his apprenticeship coincided with the heyday of New Criticism, a way of reading and writing poetry that favored irony, wit, dexterity, constraint, and subtlety. Those qualities are all on display in his first book. There is a gallantry of formal design, and an almost baroque excess of poetic language and learning. There are few short poems, because from the start Hecht preferred to dramatize, digress, and slowly divulge. His motifs— a fountain, say, or a cat—are *moving* objects in an intricate balance or a controlled disorder. And lurking behind most of the poems is a sense of mortality, the flesh as the skeleton's carnival mask.

When *The Hard Hours* appeared thirteen years later, a clutch of poems from *A Summoning of Stones* was reprinted at the end of the new collection, but the effect was less to remember an earlier achievement than to emphasize what an advance the new poems represented. The book opens with "A Hill," one of his strongest poems, an eerie account of the long cold arm of trauma as it reaches into a man's life. The contrasting panels of this poem—a sunlit clarity and a chilling shadow—are everywhere echoed in the rest of the book, but Hecht's desire here is not merely to depict them but to understand their dynamics. His style has drawn closer to speech, and the dramatic appeal of the poems is more skillfully managed. The tone can be wry, but the gravity is more fierce and compelling. Other poems in the book—"Third Avenue in Sunlight," say, or "Behold the Lilies of the Field"—explore the borders of sanity, linking the history of humankind with the individual psyche, each an emblem of the other. Still other poems return to feelings elicited by his wartime experiences in Europe. " 'More Light! More Light!' " surely ranks with Auden's "The Shield of Achilles" as one of the most disquieting poems of the century, their portraits of war all the more terrible for the restraint of the telling. The centerpiece of *The Hard Hours* is another poem that comes from the darkest hours in Hecht's own life, his encounter as a battle-weary infantryman with the German concentration camps at the end of World War II. "Rites and Ceremonies" is unlike any other Hecht poem, and the reader is aware of the wrenching emotional cost to the poet as he put the pieces together: suffering, prayer, brutality, despair. Rather than the steady voice of other Hecht poems, this poem is a collage of Biblical and liturgical fragments juxtaposed with what seem black-and-white glimpses of a documentary film about man's inhumanity to man.

After a ten-year silence, two books appeared in quick succession, *Millions of Strange Shadows* (1977) and *The Venetian Vespers* (1979), and can be read together as the next stage of his poetic development. Now, his dramatic instincts dominate, and there is a remarkable new amplitude to these books, a hovering sympathy with thwarted desire. His tone can be sadly ironic, as in the chambermaid's tale that gives "The Grapes" its pathos; or it can be more tautly heartbreaking, as in the masterful "Coming Home," about the English pastoral poet John Clare's attempted escape from a mental asylum, an escape that only leads him into a deeper confusion and loss. The profound sense of gratified love that animates "Peripeteia" is the obverse of the delusion and repressed rage that drive "Green: An Epistle." Hecht's virtuosity and range are at their best in these books. The longer narrative poems that anchor *The Venetian Vespers* provide exquisite evidence of this judgment. The title poem especially is a grand monologue, man at the end of his tether, the story of an empty life haunted by an unhappy childhood (Hecht himself once wrote that "for many complicated reasons my childhood was a rather bitter and lonely one") and by a glistening, grimy, glorious beauty that swirls about him in a fabled city of wavering reflections.

His final three books are a closing chapter. *The Transparent Man* includes two long poems—one of them, the spooky "See Naples and Die," about a collapsing marriage, is included here—and, in the book's title poem, one of his most eloquent dramatic monologues. But in general the poems in these collections are shorter, pungent variations on familiar themes. Hecht returns to an abiding source of inspiration, the masterpieces of the painter's art. The idiom of composition and color always attracted him, and to listen in as he describes the effects of the brush is an enlightening privilege. Also, whether translating a chorus by the old Sophocles or revisiting episodes in the Bible, he writes here from the perspective of age. There is an achieved wisdom to many of these later poems, condensed rather than garrulous, sometimes sardonic, sometimes severe. "The Presumptions of Death" is a witty set of assumptions, the poet putting Death through his paces in order to dramatize the roles *we* play seeking to avoid the inevitable. Yet there is never the sense of lines engraved in granite. His wit and curiosity, the warmth of his affections, and the chiaroscuro rendering of his scenes, his ability to startle—all these remain. The late poems are quieter, reconciled, more accepting, and in poems like "Devotions of a Painter," "Prospects," "Proust on

Skates," "Late Afternoon," and "The Darkness and the Light Are Both Alike to Thee," the redemptive power of beauty is celebrated with a renewed urgency.

For over half a century, poets and readers alike have turned to these books for their technical mastery, their intellectual power, and the plenitude of their emotion. If I had to single out one of his literary achievements that I value most, it would be his truth-telling—his steady, clear-eyed confrontation with the facts of our lives. I would not want to underestimate the salty slang, the satiric bite, or the ingenious wit of some of his poems. But I return with gratitude to that strain in Hecht's work, so rare in contemporary poetry, that I can only call *noble*—high, important matters dealt with in a manner that is contained, dignified, and open, full of feeling: life looked at from the vantage of spirit.

J. D. McClatchy

from A SUMMONING OF STONES

DOUBLE SONNET

I recall everything, but more than all,
Words being nothing now, an ease that ever
Remembers her to my unfailing fever,
How she came forward to me, letting fall
Lamplight upon her dress till every small
Motion made visible seemed no mere endeavor
Of body to articulate its offer,
But more a grace won by the way from all
Striving in what is difficult, from all
Losses, so that she moved but to discover
A practice of the blood, as the gulls hover,
Winged with their life, above the harbor wall,
Tracing inflected silence in the tall
Air with a tilt of mastery and quiver
Against the light, as the light fell to favor
Her coming forth; this chiefly I recall.

It is a part of pride, guiding the hand
At the piano in the splash and passage
Of sacred dolphins, making numbers human
By sheer extravagance that can command
Pythagorean heavens to spell their message
Of some unlooked-for peace, out of the common;
Taking no thought at all that man and woman,
Lost in the trance of lamplight, felt the presage
Of the unbidden terror and bone hand
Of gracelessness, and the unspoken omen
That yet shall render all, by its first usage,
Speechless, inept, and totally unmanned.

It was a miniature country once
To my imagination; Home of the Short,
And also the academy of stunts
    Where acrobats are taught
  The famous secrets of the trade:
  To cycle in the big parade
While spinning plates upon their parasols,
Or somersaults that do not touch the ground,
    Or tossing seven balls
In Most Celestial Order round and round.

A child's quick sense of the ingenious stamped
All their invention: toys I used to get
At Christmastime, or the peculiar, cramped
    Look of their alphabet.
  Fragile and easily destroyed,
  Those little boats of celluloid
Driven by camphor round the bathroom sink,
And delicate the folded paper prize
    Which, dropped into a drink
Of water, grew up right before your eyes.

Now when we reached them it was with a sense
Sharpened for treachery compounding in their brains
Like mating weasels; our Intelligence
    Said: The Black Dragon reigns
  Secretly under yellow skin,
  Deeper than dyes of atabrine
And deadlier. The War Department said:
Remember you are Americans; forsake
    The wounded and the dead
At your own cost; remember Pearl and Wake.

And yet they bowed us in with ceremony,
Told us what brands of Sake were the best,
Explained their agriculture in a phony
  Dialect of the West,

  Meant vaguely to be understood
  As a shy sign of brotherhood
In the old human bondage to the facts
Of day-to-day existence. And like ants,
    Signalling tiny pacts
With their antennae, they would wave their hands.

At last we came to see them not as glib
Walkers of tightropes, worshippers of carp,
Nor yet a species out of Adam's rib
    Meant to preserve its warp
  In Cain's own image. They had learned
  That their tough eye-born goddess burned
Adoring fingers. They were very poor.
The holy mountain was not moved to speak.
    Wind at the paper door
Offered them snow out of its hollow peak.

Human endeavor clumsily betrays
Humanity. Their excrement served in this;
For, planting rice in water, they would raise
    Schistosomiasis
  Japonica, that enters through
  The pores into the avenue
And orbit of the blood, where it may foil
The heart and kill, or settle in the brain.
    This fruit of their nightsoil
Thrives in the skull, where it is called insane.

Now the quaint early image of Japan
That was so charming to me as a child
Seems like a bright design upon a fan,
    Of water rushing wild
   On rocks that can be folded up,
   A river which the wrist can stop
With a neat flip, revealing merely sticks
And silk of what had been a fan before,
    And like such winning tricks,
It shall be buried in excelsior.

SAMUEL SEWALL

Samuel Sewall, in a world of wigs,
Flouted opinion in his personal hair;
For foppery he gave not any figs,
But in his right and honor took the air.

Thus in his naked style, though well attired,
He went forth in the city, or paid court
To Madam Winthrop, whom he much admired,
Most godly, but yet liberal with the port.

And all the town admired for two full years
His excellent address, his gifts of fruit,
Her gracious ways and delicate white ears,
And held the course of nature absolute.

But yet she bade him suffer a peruke,
"That One be not distinguished from the All";
Delivered of herself this stern rebuke
Framed in the resonant language of St. Paul.

"Madam," he answered her, "I have a Friend
Furnishes me with hair out of His strength,
And He requires only I attend
Unto His charity and to its length."

And all the town was witness to his trust:
On Monday he walked out with the Widow Gibbs,
A pious lady of charm and notable bust,
Whose heart beat tolerably beneath her ribs.

On Saturday he wrote proposing marriage,
And closed, imploring that she be not cruel,
"Your favorable answer will oblige,
Madam, your humble servant, Samuel Sewall."

Held in her hand of "almost flawless skin"
A small sprig of Sweet William as a badge
Of beauty, and the region of her nose
Seemed to be made so delicate and thin,
Light of the sun might touch the cartilage
With numerous golden tones and hints of rose
If she but turned to the window now to smell
The lilacs and the undulant green lawn,
Trim as a golf course, where a haze revealed
The sheep, distinguished each with a separate bell,
Grazing and moping near the neighbor field
Where all the clover-seeking bees were gone,
But stood in modesty in the full sight
Of Memling, whose accomplished busy hand
Rendered this wimpled lady in such white
Untinted beauty, that she seems to stand
Even as gently to our present gaze
As she had stood there in her breathing days.

Seeing this painting, I am put in mind
Of many a freakish harridan and clown
Who by their native clumsiness or fate
Won for themselves astonishing renown
And stand amongst us even to this date
Since art and history were so inclined:
Here, in a generous Italian scene,
A pimpled, chinless shepherd, whose rough thought
And customary labor lead the ram
Into his sheep for profit and for sport,
Guide their ungainly pleasure with obscene
Mirth at the comedy of sire and dam
Till he has grossly married every ewe—
This shepherd, in a mangy cap of fur,
Stands at the window still regarding her,
That only lady, if the Pope speaks true,
Who with a grace more than we understand
Ate of her portion with a flawless hand.

And once a chattering agent of Pope Paul,
A small, foul-minded clergyman, stood by
To watch the aging Michelangelo
Set his *Last Judgment* on the papal wall,
And muttered thereupon that to his eye
It was a lewd and most indecent show
Of nakedness, not for a sacred place,
Fitted to whorehouse or to public bath;
At which the painter promptly drew his face
Horribly gripped, his face a fist of pain,
Amongst those fixed in God's eternal wrath,
And when the fool made motion to complain
He earned this solemn judgment of the Pope:
"Had art set you on Purgatory's Mount
Then had I done my utmost for your hope,
But Hell's fierce immolation takes no count
Of offices and prayers, for as you know,
From that place *nulla est redemptio.*"

And I recall certain ambassadors,
Cuffed all in ermine and with vests of mail,
Who came their way into the town of Prague
Announced by horns, as history tells the tale,
To seek avoidances of future wars
And try the meaning of the Decalogue,
But whispers went about against their names.
And so it happened that a courtier-wit,
Hating their cause with an intemperate might,
Lauded his castle's vantage, and made claims
Upon their courtesy to visit it,
And having brought them to that famous height
To witness the whole streamed and timbered view
Of his ancestral property, and smell
His fine ancestral air, he pushed them through
The open-standing window, whence they fell,
 Oh, in a manner worthy to be sung,
 Full thirty feet into a pile of dung.

How many poets, with profoundest breath,
Have set their ladies up to spite the worm,
So that pale mistress or high-busted bawd
Could smile and spit into the eye of death
And dance into our midst all fleshed and firm
Despite she was most perishably flawed?
She lasts, but not in her own body's right,
Nor do we love her for her endless poise.
All of her beauty has become a part
Of neighboring beauty, and what could excite
High expectations among hopeful boys
Now leaves her to the nunnery of art.
And yet a searching discipline can keep
That eye still clear, as though in spite of Hell,
So that she seems as innocent as sheep
Where they still graze, denuded of their smell,
Where fool still writhes upon the chapel wall,
A shepherd stares, ambassadors still fall.

Adam and Eve knew such perfection once,
God's finger in the cloud, and on the ground
Nothing but springtime, nothing else at all.
But in our fallen state where the blood hunts
For blood, and rises at the hunting sound,
What do we know of lasting since the fall?
Who has not, in the oil and heat of youth,
Thought of the flourishing of the almond tree,
The grasshopper, and the failing of desire,
And thought his tongue might pierce the secrecy
Of the six-pointed starlight, and might choir
A secret-voweled, unutterable truth?

The heart is ramified with an old force
(Outlingering the blood, out of the sway
Of its own fleshy trap) that finds its source
Deep in the phosphorous waters of the bay,
Or in the wind, or pointing cedar tree,
Or its own ramified complexity.

CHRISTMAS IS COMING

Darkness is for the poor, and thorough cold,
As they go wandering the hills at night,
Gunning for enemies. Winter locks the lake;
The rocks are harder for it. What was grass
Is fossilized and brittle; it can hurt,
Being a torture to the kneeling knee,
And in the general pain of cold, it sticks
Particular pain where crawling is required.

> *Christmas is coming. The goose is getting fat.*
> *Please put a penny in the Old Man's hat.*

Where is the warmth of blood? The enemy
Has ears that can hear clearly in the cold,
Can hear the shattering of fossil grass,
Can hear the stiff cloth rub against itself,
Making a sound. Where is the blood? It lies
Locked in the limbs of some poor animal
In a diaspora of crimson ice.
The skin freezes to metal. One must crawl
Quietly in the dark. Where is the warmth?
The lamb has yielded up its fleece and warmth
And woolly life, but who shall taste of it?
Here on the ground one cannot see the stars.
The lamb is killed. *The goose is getting fat.*
A wind blows steadily against the trees,
And somewhere in the blackness they are black.
Yet crawling one encounters bits of string,
Pieces of foil left by the enemy.
(A rifle takes its temper from the cold.)
Where is the pain? The sense has frozen up,
And fingers cannot recognize the grass,
Cannot distinguish their own character,
Being blind with cold, being stiffened by the cold;
Must find out thistles to remember pain.
Keep to the frozen ground or else be killed.
Yet crawling one encounters in the dark

The frosty carcasses of birds, their feet
And wings all glazed. And still we crawl to learn
Where pain was lost, how to recover pain.
Reach for the brambles, crawl to them and reach,
Clutching for thorns, search carefully to feel
The point of thorns, life's crown, *the Old Man's hat*.
Yet quietly. Do not disturb the brambles.
Winter has taught the air to clarify
All noises, and the enemy can hear
Perfectly in the cold. Nothing but sound
Is known. Where is the warmth and pain?
Christmas is coming. Darkness is for the poor.

> *If you haven't got a penny, a ha'penny will do,*
> *If you haven't got a ha'penny, God bless you.*

This is Italian. Here
Is cause for the undiminished bounce
Of sex, cause for the lark, the animal spirit
To rise, aerated, but not beyond our reach, to spread
Friction upon the air, cause to sing loud for the bed
Of jonquils, the linen bed, and established merit
Of love, and grandly to pronounce
Pleasure without peer.

Goddess, be with me now;
Commend my music to the woods.
There is no garden to the practiced gaze
Half so erotic: here the sixteenth-century thew
Rose to its last perfection, this being chiefly due
To the provocative role the water plays.
Tumble and jump, the fountains' moods
Teach the world how.

But, ah, who ever saw
Finer proportion kept. The sum
Of intersecting limbs was something planned.
Ligorio, the laurel! Every turn and quirk
Weaves in this waving green and liquid world to work
Its formula, binding upon the gland,
Even as molecules succumb
To Avogadro's law.

The intricate mesh of trees,
Sagging beneath a lavender snow
Of wisteria, wired by creepers, perfectly knit
A plot to capture alive the migrant, tourist soul
In its corporeal home with all the deft control
And artifice of an Hephaestus' net.
Sunlight and branch rejoice to show
Sudden interstices.

The whole garden inclines
The flesh as water falls, to seek
For depth. Consider the top balustrade,
Where twinned stone harpies, with domed and virgin breasts,
Spurt from their nipples that no pulse or hand has pressed
Clear liquid arcs of benefice and aid
To the chief purpose. They are Greek
Versions of valentines

And spend themselves to fill
The celebrated flumes that skirt
The horseshoe stairs. Triumphant then to a sluice,
With Brownian movement down the giggling water drops
Past haunches, over ledges, out of mouths, and stops
In a still pool, but, by a plumber's ruse,
Rises again to laugh and squirt
At heaven, and is still

Busy descending. White
Ejaculations leap to teach
How fertile are these nozzles; the streams run
Góngora through the garden, channel themselves, and pass
To lily-padded ease, where insubordinate lass
And lad can cool their better parts, where sun
Heats them again to furnace pitch
To prove his law is light.

Marble the fish that puke
Eternally, marble the lips
Of gushing naiads, pleased to ridicule
Adonis, marble himself, and larger than life-sized,
Untouched by Venus, posthumously circumcised
Patron of Purity; and any fool
Who feels no flooding at the hips
These spendthrift stones rebuke.

It was in such a place
That Mozart's Figaro contrived
The totally expected. This is none
Of your French topiary, geometric works,
Based on God's rational, wrist-watch universe; here lurks
The wood louse, the night crawler, the homespun
Spider; here are they born and wived
And bedded, by God's grace.

Actually, it is real
The way the world is real: the horse
Must turn against the wind, and the deer feed
Against the wind, and finally the garden must allow
For the recalcitrant; a style can teach us how
To know the world in little where the weed
Has license, where by dint of force
D'Estes have set their seal.

Their spirit entertains.
And we are honorable guests
Come by imagination, come by night,
Hearing in the velure of darkness impish strings
Mincing Tartini, hearing the hidden whisperings:
"*Carissima*, the moon gives too much light,"
Though by its shining it invests
Her bodice with such gains

As show their shadowed worth
Deep in the cleavage. Lanterns, lamps
Of pumpkin-colored paper dwell upon
The implications of the skin-tight silk, allude
Directly to the body; under the subdued
Report of corks, whisperings, the *chaconne*,
Boisterous water runs its ramps
Out, to the end of mirth.

Accommodating plants
Give umbrage where the lovers delve
Deeply for love, give way to their delight,
As Pliny's pregnant mouse, bearing unborn within her
Lewd sons and pregnant daughters, hears the adept beginner:
"*Cor mio,* your supports are much too tight,"
While overhead the stars resolve
Every extravagance.

Tomorrow, before dawn,
Gardeners will come to resurrect
Downtrodden iris, dispose of broken glass,
Return the diamond earrings to the villa, but
As for the moss upon the statue's shoulder, not
To defeat its green invasion, but to pass
Over the liberal effect
Caprice and cunning spawn.

For thus it was designed:
Controlled disorder at the heart
Of everything, the paradox, the old
Oxymoronic itch to set the formal strictures
Within a natural context, where the tension lectures
Us on our mortal state, and by controlled
Disorder, labors to keep art
From being too refined.

Susan, it had been once
My hope to see this place with you,
See it as in the hour of thoughtless youth.
For age mocks all diversity, its genesis,
And whispers to the heart, "*Cor mio,* beyond all this
Lies the unchangeable and abstract truth,"
Claims of the grass, it is not true,
And makes our youth its dunce.

Therefore, some later day
Recall these words, let them be read
Between us, let them signify that here
Are more than formulas, that age sees no more clearly
For its poor eyesight, and philosophy grows surly,
That falling water and the blood's career
Lead down the garden path to bed
And win us both to May.

ALCESTE IN THE WILDERNESS

Non, je ne puis souffrir cette lâche méthode
Qu' affectent la plupart de vos gens à la mode . . .
                    —MOLIÈRE: *Le Misanthrope*

Evening is clogged with gnats as the light fails,
And branches bloom with gold and copper screams
Of birds with figured and sought-after tails
To plume a lady's gear; the motet wails
Through Africa upon dissimilar themes.

A little snuffbox whereon Daphnis sings
In pale enamels, touching love's defeat,
Calls up the color of her underthings
And plays upon the taut memorial strings,
Trailing her laces down into this heat.

One day he found, topped with a smutty grin,
The small corpse of a monkey, partly eaten.
Force of the sun had split the bluish skin,
Which, by their questioning and entering in,
A swarm of bees had been concerned to sweeten.

He could distill no essence out of this.
That yellow majesty and molten light
Should bless this carcass with a sticky kiss
Argued a brute and filthy emphasis.
The half-moons of the fingernails were white,

And where the nostrils opened on the skies,
Issuing to the sinus, where the ant
Crawled swiftly down to undermine the eyes
Of cloudy aspic, nothing could disguise
How terribly the thing looked like Philinte.

Will-o'-the-wisp, on the scum-laden water,
Burns in the night, a gaseous deceiver,
In the pale shade of France's foremost daughter.
Heat gives his thinking cavity no quarter,
For he is burning with the monkey's fever.

Before the bees have diagrammed their comb
Within the skull, before summer has cracked
The back of Daphnis, naked, polychrome,
Versailles shall see the tempered exile home,
Peruked and stately for the final act.

from THE HARD HOURS

A HILL

In Italy, where this sort of thing can occur,
I had a vision once—though you understand
It was nothing at all like Dante's, or the visions of saints,
And perhaps not a vision at all. I was with some friends,
Picking my way through a warm sunlit piazza
In the early morning. A clear fretwork of shadows
From huge umbrellas littered the pavement and made
A sort of lucent shallows in which was moored
A small navy of carts. Books, coins, old maps,
Cheap landscapes and ugly religious prints
Were all on sale. The colors and noise
Like the flying hands were gestures of exultation,
So that even the bargaining
Rose to the ear like a voluble godliness.
And then, when it happened, the noises suddenly stopped,
And it got darker; pushcarts and people dissolved
And even the great Farnese Palace itself
Was gone, for all its marble; in its place
Was a hill, mole-colored and bare. It was very cold,
Close to freezing, with a promise of snow.
The trees were like old ironwork gathered for scrap
Outside a factory wall. There was no wind,
And the only sound for a while was the little click
Of ice as it broke in the mud under my feet.
I saw a piece of ribbon snagged on a hedge,
But no other sign of life. And then I heard
What seemed the crack of a rifle. A hunter, I guessed;
At least I was not alone. But just after that
Came the soft and papery crash
Of a great branch somewhere unseen falling to earth.

And that was all, except for the cold and silence
That promised to last forever, like the hill.

Then prices came through, and fingers, and I was restored
To the sunlight and my friends. But for more than a week
I was scared by the plain bitterness of what I had seen.
All this happened about ten years ago,
And it hasn't troubled me since, but at last, today,
I remembered that hill; it lies just to the left
Of the road north of Poughkeepsie; and as a boy
I stood before it for hours in wintertime.

THIRD AVENUE IN SUNLIGHT

Third Avenue in sunlight. Nature's error.
Already the bars are filled and John is there.
Beneath a plentiful lady over the mirror
He tilts his glass in the mild mahogany air.

I think of him when he first got out of college,
Serious, thin, unlikely to succeed;
For several months he hung around the Village,
Boldly T-shirted, unfettered but unfreed.

Now he confides to a stranger, "I was first scout,
And kept my glimmers peeled till after dark.
Our outfit had as its sign a bloody knout,
We met behind the museum in Central Park.

Of course, we were kids." But still those savages,
War-painted, a flap of leather at the loins,
File silently against him. Hostages
Are never taken. One summer, in Des Moines,

They entered his hotel room, tomahawks
Flashing like barracuda. He tried to pray.
Three years of treatment. Occasionally he talks
About how he almost didn't get away.

Daily the prowling sunlight whets its knife
Along the sidewalk. We almost never meet.
In the Rembrandt dark he lifts his amber life.
My bar is somewhat further down the street.

TARANTULA OR THE DANCE OF DEATH

During the plague I came into my own.
It was a time of smoke-pots in the house
Against infection. The blind head of bone
                    Grinned its abuse

Like a good democrat at everyone.
Runes were recited daily, charms were applied.
That was the time I came into my own.
                    Half Europe died.

The symptoms are a fever and dark spots
First on the hands, then on the face and neck,
But even before the body, the mind rots.
                    You can be sick

Only a day with it before you're dead.
But the most curious part of it is the dance.
The victim goes, in short, out of his head.
                    A sort of trance

Glazes the eyes, and then the muscles take
His will away from him, the legs begin
Their funeral jig, the arms and belly shake
                    Like souls in sin.

Some, caught in these convulsions, have been known
To fall from windows, fracturing the spine.
Others have drowned in streams. The smooth headstone,
                    The box of pine,

Are not for the likes of these. Moreover, flame
Is powerless against contagion.
That was the black winter when I came
                    Into my own.

THE END OF THE WEEKEND

A dying firelight slides along the quirt
Of the cast-iron cowboy where he leans
Against my father's books. The lariat
Whirls into darkness. My girl, in skin-tight jeans,
Fingers a page of Captain Marryat,
Inviting insolent shadows to her shirt.

We rise together to the second floor.
Outside, across the lake, an endless wind
Whips at the headstones of the dead and wails
In the trees for all who have and have not sinned.
She rubs against me and I feel her nails.
Although we are alone, I lock the door.

The eventual shapes of all our formless prayers,
This dark, this cabin of loose imaginings,
Wind, lake, lip, everything awaits
The slow unloosening of her underthings.
And then the noise. Something is dropped. It grates
Against the attic beams.
                              I climb the stairs,

Armed with a belt.
                         A long magnesium strip
Of moonlight from the dormer cuts a path
Among the shattered skeletons of mice.
A great black presence beats its wings in wrath.
Above the boneyard burn its golden eyes.
Some small grey fur is pulsing in its grip.

It is raining here.
On my neighbor's fire escape
geraniums are set out
in their brick-clay pots,
along with the mop,
old dishrags, and a cracked
enamel bowl for the dog.

I think of you out there
on the sandy edge of things,
rain strafing the beach,
the white maturity
of bones and broken shells,
and little tin shovels and cars
rusting under the house.

And between us there is—what?
Love and constraint,
conditions, conditions,
and several hundred miles
of billboards, filling-stations,
and little dripping gardens.
The fir tree full of whispers,
trinkets of water,
the bob, duck, and release
of the weighted rose,
life in the freshened stones.
(They used to say that rain
is good for growing boys,
and once I stood out in it
hoping to rise a foot.
The biggest drops fattened
on the gutters under the eaves,
sidled along the slant,
picked up speed, let go,

and met their dooms in a "plock"
beside my gleaming shins.
I must have been near the size
of your older son.)

Yesterday was nice.
I took my boys to the park.
We played Ogre on the grass.
I am, of course, the Ogre,
and invariably get killed.
Merciless and barefooted,
they sneak up from behind
and they let me have it.

O my dear, my dear,
today the rain pummels
the sour geraniums
and darkens the grey pilings
of your house, built upon sand.
And both of us, full grown,
have weathered a long year.
Perhaps your casual glance
will settle from time to time
on the sea's travelling muscles
that flex and roll their strength
under its rain-pocked skin.
And you'll see where the salt winds
have blown bare the seaward side
of the berry bushes,
and will notice
the faint, fresh
smell of iodine.

BEHOLD THE LILIES OF THE FIELD

for Leonard Baskin

And now. An attempt.
Don't tense yourself; take it easy.
Look at the flowers there in the glass bowl.
Yes, they are lovely and fresh. I remember
Giving my mother flowers once, rather like those
(Are they narcissus or jonquils?),
And I hoped she would show some pleasure in them
But got that mechanical enthusiastic show
She used on the telephone once in praising some friend
For thoughtfulness or good taste or whatever it was,
And when she hung up, turned to us all and said,
"God, what a bore she is!"
I think she was trying to show us how honest she was,
At least with us. But the effect
Was just the opposite, and now I don't think
She knows what honesty is. "Your mother's a whore,"
Someone said, not meaning she slept around,
Though perhaps this was part of it, but
Meaning she had lost all sense of honor,
And I think this is true.

But that's not what I wanted to say.
What was it I wanted to say?
When he said that about Mother, I had to laugh,
I really did, it was so amazingly true.
Where was I?
Lie back. Relax.
Oh yes. I remember now what it was.
It was what I saw them do to the emperor.
They captured him, you know. Eagles and all.
They stripped him, and made an iron collar for his neck,
And they made a cage out of our captured spears,
And they put him inside, naked and collared,
And exposed to the view of the whole enemy camp.
And I was tied to a post and made to watch
When he was taken out and flogged by one of their generals

And then forced to offer his ripped back
As a mounting block for the barbarian king
To get on his horse;
And one time to get down on all fours to be the royal throne
When the king received our ambassadors
To discuss the question of ransom.
Of course, he didn't want ransom.
And I was tied to a post and made to watch.
That's enough for now. Lie back. Try to relax.
No, that's not all.
They kept it up for two months.
We were taken to their outmost provinces.
It was always the same, and we were always made to watch,
The others and I. How he stood it, I don't know.
And then suddenly
There were no more floggings or humiliations,
The king's personal doctor saw to his back,
He was given decent clothing, and the collar was taken off,
And they treated us all with a special courtesy.
By the time we reached their capital city
His back was completely healed.
They had taken the cage apart—
But of course they didn't give us back our spears.
Then later that month, it was a warm afternoon in May,
The rest of us were marched out to the central square.
The crowds were there already, and the posts were set up,
To which we were tied in the old watching positions.
And he was brought out in the old way, and stripped,
And then tied flat on a big rectangular table
So that only his head could move.
Then the king made a short speech to the crowds,
To which they responded with gasps of wild excitement,
And which was then translated for the rest of us.
It was the sentence. He was to be flayed alive,
As slowly as possible, to drag out the pain.
And we were made to watch. The king's personal doctor,

The one who had tended his back,
Came forward with a tray of surgical knives.
They began at the feet.
And we were not allowed to close our eyes
Or to look away. When they were done, hours later,
The skin was turned over to one of their saddle-makers
To be tanned and stuffed and sewn. And for what?
A hideous life-sized doll, filled out with straw,
In the skin of the Roman Emperor, Valerian,
With blanks of mother-of-pearl under the eyelids,
And painted shells that had been prepared beforehand
For the fingernails and toenails,
Roughly cross-stitched on the inseam of the legs
And up the back to the center of the head,
Swung in the wind on a rope from the palace flag-pole;
And young girls were brought there by their mothers
To be told about the male anatomy.
His death had taken hours.
They were very patient.
And with him passed away the honor of Rome.

In the end, I was ransomed. Mother paid for me.
You must rest now. You must. Lean back.
Look at the flowers.
Yes. I am looking. I wish I could be like them.

THE DOVER BITCH

A Criticism of Life

for Andrews Wanning

So there stood Matthew Arnold and this girl
With the cliffs of England crumbling away behind them,
And he said to her, "Try to be true to me,
And I'll do the same for you, for things are bad
All over, etc., etc."
Well now, I knew this girl. It's true she had read
Sophocles in a fairly good translation
And caught that bitter allusion to the sea,
But all the time he was talking she had in mind
The notion of what his whiskers would feel like
On the back of her neck. She told me later on
That after a while she got to looking out
At the lights across the channel, and really felt sad,
Thinking of all the wine and enormous beds
And blandishments in French and the perfumes.
And then she got really angry. To have been brought
All the way down from London, and then be addressed
As a sort of mournful cosmic last resort
Is really tough on a girl, and she was pretty.
Anyway, she watched him pace the room
And finger his watch-chain and seem to sweat a bit,
And then she said one or two unprintable things.
But you mustn't judge her by that. What I mean to say is,
She's really all right. I still see her once in a while
And she always treats me right. We have a drink
And I give her a good time, and perhaps it's a year
Before I see her again, but there she is,
Running to fat, but dependable as they come.
And sometimes I bring her a bottle of *Nuit d'Amour.*

THREE PROMPTERS FROM THE WINGS

for George and Mary Dimock

ATROPOS: OR, THE FUTURE

He rushed out of the temple
And for all his young good looks,
Excellence at wrestling,
High and manly pride,
The giddy world's own darling,
He thought of suicide.
(The facts are clear and simple
But are not found in books.)

Think how the young suppose
That any minute now
Some darkly beautiful
Stranger's leg or throat
Will speak out in the taut
Inflections of desire,
Will choose them, will allow
Each finger its own thought
And whatever it reaches for.
A vision without clothes
Tickles the genitalia
And makes blithe the heart.
But in this most of all
He was cut out for failure.

That morning smelled of hay.
But all that he found tempting
Was a high, weathered cliff.
Now at a subtle prompting
He hesitated. If
He ended down below
He had overcome the Fates;
The oracle was false;
The gods themselves were blind.

A fate he could contravene
Was certainly not Fate.
All lay in his power.
(How this came to his mind
No child of man can say.
The clear, rational light
Touches on less than half,
And "he who hesitates . . ."
For who could presume to know
The decisive, inward pulse
Of things?)
　　　　　After an hour
He rose to his full height,
The master of himself.

That morning smelled of hay,
The day was clear. A moisture
Cooled at the tips of leaves.
The fields were overlaid
With light. It was harvest time.
Three swallows appraised the day,
And bearing aloft their lives,
Sailed into a wild climb,
Then spilled across the pasture
Like water over tiles.
One could have seen for miles
The sun on a knife-blade.
And there he stood, the hero,
With a lascivious wind
Sliding across his chest.
(The sort of thing that women,
Who are fools the whole world over,
Would fondle and adore

And stand before undressed.)
But deep within his loins
A bitterness is set.
He is already blind.

The faceless powers summon
To their eternal sorrow
The handsome, bold, and vain,
And those dark things are met
At a place where three roads join.
They touch with an open sore
The lips that he shall kiss.
And some day men may call me,
Because I'm old and plain
And never had a lover,
The authoress of this.

CLOTHO: OR, THE PRESENT

Well, there he stands, surrounded
By all his kith and kin,
Townspeople and friends,
As the evidence rolls in,
And don't go telling me
The spectacle isn't silly.

A prince in low disguise,
Moving among the humble
With kingly purposes,
Is an old, romantic posture,
And always popular.
He started on this career
By overthrowing Fate
(A splendid accomplishment,
And all done in an hour)

That crucial day at the temple
When the birds crossed over the pasture
As was said by my sister, here.
Which goes to show that an omen
Is a mere tissue of lies
To please the superstitious
And keep the masses content.
From this initial success
He moved on without pause
To outwit and subdue a vicious
Beast with lion's paws,
The wings of a great bird,
And the breasts and face of a woman.
This meant knowing no less
Than the universal state
Of man. Which is quite a lot.
(Construe this as you please.)

Now today an old abuse
Raises its head and festers
To the scandal and disease
Of all. He will weed it out
And cleanse the earth of it.
Clearly, if anyone could,
He can redeem these lands;
To doubt this would be absurd.
The finest faculties,
Courage and will and wit,
He has patiently put to use
For Truth and the Common Good,
And lordly above the taunts
Of his enemies, there he stands,
The father of his sisters,
His daughters their own aunts.

Some sentimental fool
Invented the Tragic Muse.

She doesn't exist at all.
For human life is composed
In reasonably equal parts
Of triumph and chagrin,
And the parts are so hotly fused
As to seem a single thing.
This is true as well
Of wisdom and ignorance
And of happiness and pain:
Nothing is purely itself
But is linked with its antidote
In cold self-mockery—
A fact with which only those
Born with a Comic sense
Can learn to content themselves.
While heroes die to maintain
Some part of existence clean
And incontaminate.

Now take this fellow here
Who is about to find
The summit of his life
Founded upon disaster.
Lovers can learn as much
Every night in bed,
For whatever flesh can touch
Is never quite enough.
They know it is tempting fate
To hold out for perfect bliss.
And yet the whole world over
Blind men will choose as master
To lead them the most blind.
And some day men may call me,
Because I'm old and tough,
And never had a lover,
The instrument of this.

Well, now. You might suppose
There's nothing left to be said.
Outcast, corrupt and blind,
He knows it's night when an owl
Wakes up to hoot at the wise,
And the owl inside his head
Looks out of sightless eyes,
Answers, and sinks its toes
Into the soft and bloody
Center of his mind.

But miles and miles away
Suffers another man.
He was young, open-hearted,
Strong in mind and body
When all these things began.
Every blessed night
He attends the moonstruck owl,
Familiar of the witless,
And remembers a dark day,
A new-born baby's howl,
And an autumnal wetness.

The smallest sign of love
Is always an easy target
For the jealous and cynical.
Perhaps, indeed, they are right.
I leave it for you to say.
But to leave a little child,
Roped around the feet,
To the charities of a wolf
Was more than he could stomach.
He weighed this for an hour,
Then rose to his full height,

The master of himself.
And the last, clinching witness.
The great life he spared
He would return to punish
And punish himself as well.

But recently his woes
Are muted by the moon.
He no longer goes alone.
Thorns have befriended him,
And once he found his mother
Hiding under a stone.
She was fat, wet, and lame.
She said it was clever of him
To find her in the dark
But he always had been a wise one,
And warned him against snails.
And now his every word
Is free of all human hates
And human kindliness.
To be mad, as the world goes,
Is not the worst of fates.
(And please do not forget
There are those who find this comic.)

But what, you ask, of the hero?
(Ah well, I am very old
And they say I have a rambling
Or a devious sort of mind.)
At midnight and in rain
He advances without trembling
From sorrow unto sorrow
Toward a kind of light
The sun makes upon metal
Which perhaps even the blind
May secretly behold.

What the intelligence
Works out in pure delight
The body must learn in pain.
He has solved the Sphinx's riddle
In his own ligaments.

And now in a green place,
Holy and unknown,
He has taken off his clothes.
Dust in the sliding light
Swims and is gone. Fruit
Thickens. The listless cello
Of flies tuning in shadows,
Wet bark and the silver click
Of water over stones
Are close about him where
He stands, an only witness
With no eyes in his face.
In spite of which he knows
Clear as he once had known,
Though bound both hand and foot,
The smell of mountain air
And an autumnal wetness.
And he sees, moreover,
Unfolding into the light
Three pairs of wings in flight,
Moving as water moves.
The strength, wisdom and bliss
Of their inhuman loves
They scatter near the temple.
And some day men may call me,
Because I'm old and simple
And never had a lover,
Responsible for this.

THE VOW

In the third month, a sudden flow of blood.
The mirth of tabrets ceaseth, and the joy
Also of the harp. The frail image of God
Lay spilled and formless. Neither girl nor boy,
But yet blood of my blood, nearly my child.
                    All that long day
Her pale face turned to the window's mild
                    Featureless grey.

And for some nights she whimpered as she dreamed
The dead thing spoke, saying: "Do not recall
Pleasure at my conception. I am redeemed
From pain and sorrow. Mourn rather for all
Who breathlessly issue from the bone gates,
                    The gates of horn,
For truly it is best of all the fates
                    Not to be born.

"Mother, a child lay gasping for bare breath
On Christmas Eve when Santa Claus had set
Death in the stocking, and the lights of death
Flamed in the tree. O, if you can, forget
You were the child, turn to my father's lips
                    Against the time
When his cold hand puts forth its fingertips
                    Of jointed lime."

Doctors of Science, what is man that he
Should hope to come to a good end? *The best
Is not to have been born.* And could it be
That Jewish diligence and Irish jest
The consent of flesh and a midwinter storm
                    Had reconciled,
Was yet too bold a mixture to inform
                    A simple child?

Even as gold is tried, Gentile and Jew.
If that ghost was a girl's, I swear to it:
Your mother shall be far more blessed than you.
And if a boy's, I swear: The flames are lit
That shall refine us; they shall not destroy
                    A living hair.
Your younger brothers shall confirm in joy
                    This that I swear.

RITES AND CEREMONIES

I   THE ROOM

Father, Adonoi, author of all things,
       of the three states,
the soft light on the barn at dawn,
       a wind that sings
in the bracken, fire in iron grates,
       the ram's horn,
Furnisher, hinger of heaven, who bound
       the lovely Pleaides,
entered the perfect treasuries of the snow,
       established the round
course of the world, birth, death and disease,
       and caused to grow
veins, brain, bones in me, to breathe and sing
       fashioned me air,
Lord, who, governing cloud and waterspout,
       O my King,
held me alive till this my forty-third year—
       in whom we doubt—
Who was that child of whom they tell
       in lauds and threnes?
whose holy name all shall pronounce
       Emmanuel,
which being interpreted means,
       "Gott mit uns"?

I saw it on their belts. A young one, dead,
Left there on purpose to get us used to the sight
When we first moved in. Helmet spilled off, head
Blond and boyish and bloody. I was scared that night.
And the sign was there,
The sign of the child, the grave, worship and loss,
Gunpowder heavy as pollen in winter air,
An Iron Cross.

It is twenty years now, Father. I have come home.
But in the camps, one can look through a huge square
Window, like an aquarium, upon a room
The size of my living room filled with human hair.
Others have shoes, or valises
Made mostly of cardboard, which once contained
Pills, fresh diapers. This is one of the places
Never explained.

Out of one trainload, about five hundred in all,
Twenty the next morning were hopelessly insane.
And some there be that have no memorial,
That are perished as though they had never been.
Made into soap.
Who now remembers "The Singing Horses of Buchenwald"?
"Above all, the saving of lives," whispered the Pope.
Die Vögelein schweigen im Walde,

But for years the screaming continued, night and day,
And the little children were suffered to come along, too.
At night, Father, in the dark, when I pray,
I am there, I am there. I am pushed through
With the others to the strange room
Without windows; whitewashed walls, cement floor.
Millions, Father, millions have come to this pass,
Which a great church has voted to "deplore."

Are the vents in the ceiling, Father, to let the spirit depart?
We are crowded in here naked, female and male.
An old man is saying a prayer. And now we start
To panic, to claw at each other, to wail
As the rubber-edged door closes on chance and choice.
He is saying a prayer for all whom this room shall kill.
"I cried unto the Lord God with my voice,
And He has heard me out His holy hill."

Small paw tracks in the snow, eloquent of a passage
Neither seen nor heard. Over the timbered hill,
Turning at the fence, and under the crisp light of winter,
In blue shadows, trailing toward the town.
Beginning at the outposts, the fox-trot of death,
Silent and visible, slipped westward from the holy original east.
Even in "our sea" on a misty Easter
Ships were discovered adrift, heavy with pepper and tea,
The whole crew dead.

Was it a judgment?

Among the heathen, the king of Tharsis, seeing
Such sudden slaughter of his people, began a journey to Avignon
With a great multitude of his nobles, to propose to the Pope
That he become a Christian and be baptized,
Thinking that he might assuage the anger of God
Upon his people for their wicked unbelief.
But when he had journeyed twenty days,
He heard the pestilence had struck among the Christians
As among other peoples. So, turning in his tracks,
He travelled no farther, but hastened to return home.
The Christians, pursuing these people from behind,
Slew about seven thousand of them.

At the horse-trough, at dusk,
In the morning among the fishbaskets,
The soft print of the dancing-master's foot.

In Marseilles, one hundred and fifty Friars Minor.
In the region of Provence, three hundred and fifty-eight
Of the Friars Preachers died in Lent.
If it was a judgment, it struck home in the houses of penitence,
The meek and the faithful were in no wise spared.
Prayer and smoke were thought a protection.
Braziers smoldered all day on the papal floors.

During this same year, there was a great mortality
Of sheep everywhere in the kingdom;
In one place and in one pasture, more than five thousand sheep
Died and became so putrified
That neither beast nor bird wanted to touch them.
And the price of everything was cheap,
Because of the fear of death.

How could it be a judgment,
The children in convulsions, the sweating and stink,
And not enough living to bury the dead?
The shepherd had abandoned his sheep.

And presently it was found to be
Not a judgment.

The old town council had first to be deposed
And a new one elected, whose views agreed
With the will of the people. And a platform erected,
Not very high, perhaps only two inches above the tallest headstone,
But easy to view. And underneath it, concealed,
The excess lumber and nails, some logs, old brooms and straw,
Piled on the ancient graves. The preparations were hasty
But thorough, they were thorough.
A visitor to that town today is directed to
The Minster. The Facade, by Erwin von Steinbach,
Is justly the most admired part of the edifice
And presents a singularly happy union
Of the style of Northern France
With the perpendicular tendency
Peculiar to German cathedrals.
No signs of the platform are left, which in any case
Was outside the town walls.
But on that day, Saturday, February 14th,
The Sabbath, and dedicated to St. Valentine,

Everyone who was not too sick was down
To watch the ceremony. The clergy,
The new town council, the students
Of the university which later gave Goethe
His degree of Doctor of Laws.
For the evidence now was in: in Berne, under torture,
Two Jews had confessed to poisoning the wells.
Wherefore throughout Europe were these platforms erected,
Even as here in the city of Strasbourg,
And the Jews assembled upon them,
Children and all, and tied together with rope.

      It is barren hereabout
           And the wind is cold,
And the sound of prayer, clamor of curse and shout,
         Is blown past the sheepfold
            Out of hearing.

     The river worms through the snow plain
          In kindless darks.
And man is born to sorrow and to pain
        As surely as the sparks
          Fly upward.

    Father, among these many souls
        Is there not one
Whom thou shalt pluck for love out of the coals?
      Look, look, they have begun
         To douse the rags.

    O that thou shouldst give dust a tongue
        To crie to thee,
And then not heare it crying! Who is strong
      When the flame eats his knee?
         O hear my prayer,

And let my cry come unto thee.
Hide not thy face.
Let there some child among us worthy be
Here to receive thy grace
And sheltering.

It is barren hereabout
And the wind is cold,
And the crack of fire, melting of prayer and shout,
Is blown past the sheepfold
Out of hearing.

III   THE DREAM

The contemplation of horror is not edifying,
Neither does it strengthen the soul.
And the gentle serenity in the paintings of martyrs,
St. Lucy, bearing her eyes on a plate,
St. Cecilia, whose pipes were the pipes of plumbing
And whose music was live steam,
The gridiron tilting lightly against the sleeve of St. Lawrence,
These, and others, bewilder and shame us.
Not all among us are of their kind.
Fear of our own imperfections,
Fear learned and inherited,
Fear shapes itself in dreams
Not more fantastic than the brute fact.

It is the first Saturday in Carnival.
There, in the Corso, homesick Du Bellay.
Yesterday it was acrobats, and a play
About Venetian magnificos, and in the interval
Bull-baiting, palm-reading, juggling, but today

The race. Observe how sad he appears to be:
Thinking perhaps of Anjou, the climbing grace
Of smoke from a neighbor's chimney, of a place
Slate-roofed and kindly. The vast majesty
Of Rome is lost on him. But not the embrace

Of the lovers. See, see young harlequins bent
On stealing kisses from their columbines.
Here are the *dolces,* here the inebriate wines
Before the seemly austerities of Lent.
The couples form tight-packed, irregular lines

On each side of the mile-long, gorgeous course.
The men have whips and sticks with bunting tied
About them. Anointed Folly and his bride
Ordain Misrule. Camel and Barbary horse
Shall feel the general mirth upon their hide.

First down the gantlet, twenty chosen asses,
Grey, Midas-eared, mild beasts receive the jeers
And clouts of the young crowd. Consort of brasses
Salutes the victor at the far end. Glasses
Are filled again, the men caress their dears,

The children shout. But who are these that stand
And shuffle shyly at the starting line?
Twenty young men, naked, except the band
Around their loins, wait for the horn's command.
Christ's Vicar chose them, and imposed his fine.

Du Bellay, poet, take no thought of them;
And yet they too are exiles, and have said
Through many generations, long since dead,
"If I forget thee, O Jerusalem, . . ."
Still, others have been scourged and buffeted

And worse. Think rather, if you must,
Of Piranesian, elegaic woes,
Rome's grand declensions, that all-but-speaking dust.
Or think of the young gallants and their lust.
Or wait for the next heat, the buffaloes.

IV   WORDS FOR THE DAY OF ATONEMENT

Merely to have survived is not an index of excellence,
Nor, given the way things go,
Even of low cunning.
Yet I have seen the wicked in great power,
And spreading himself like a green bay tree.
And the good as if they had never been;
Their voices are blown away on the winter wind.
And again we wander the wilderness
For our transgressions
Which are confessed in the daily papers.

Except the Lord of hosts had left unto us
A very small remnant,
We should have been as Sodom,
We should have been like unto Gomorrah.
And to what purpose, as the darkness closes about
And the child screams in the jellied fire,
Had best be our present concern,
Here, in this wilderness of comfort
In which we dwell.
                    Shall we now consider
The suspicious postures of our virtue,
The deformed consequences of our love,
The painful issues of our mildest acts?

Shall we ask,
Where is there one
Mad, poor and betrayed enough to find
Forgiveness for us, saying,
"None does offend,
None, I say,
None"?

Listen, listen.
But the voices are blown away.

           And yet, this light,
           The work of thy fingers, . . .

The soul is thine, and the body is thy creation:
O have compassion on thy handiwork.
The soul is thine, and the body is thine:
O deal with us according to thy name.
We come before thee relying on thy name;
O deal with us according to thy name;
For the sake of the glory of thy name;
As the gracious and merciful God is thy name.
O Lord, for thy name's sake we plead,
Forgive us our sins, though they be very great.

     It is winter as I write.
For miles the holy treasuries of snow
       Sag the still world with white,
And all soft shapes are washed from top to toe
       In pigeon-colored light.

    Tree, bush and weed maintain
Their humbled, lovely postures all day through.
      And darkly in the brain
The famous ancient questions gather: Who
      Fathered the fathering rain

That falleth in the wilderness
Where no man is, wherein there is no man;
　　　To satisfy the cress,
Knotweed and moonwort? And shall scan
　　　Our old unlawfulness?

　　　Who shall profess to understand
The diligence and purpose of the rose?
　　　Yet deep as to some gland,
A promised odor, even among these snows,
　　　Steals in like contraband.

Forgiven be the whole Congregation of the Children of Israel, and the stranger
dwelling in their midst. For all the people have inadvertently sinned.

　　　Father, I also pray
For those among us whom we know not, those
　　　Dearest to thy grace,
The saved and saving remnant, the promised third,
　　　Who in a later day
When we again are compassed about with foes,
Shall be for us a nail in thy holy place
There to abide according to thy word.

　　　Neither shall the flame
Kindle upon them, nor the fire burn
　　　A hair of them, for they
Shall be thy care when it shall come to pass,
　　　And calling on thy name
In the hot kilns and ovens, they shall turn
To thee as it is prophesied, and say,
"He shall come down like rain upon mown grass."

I have been wondering
What you are thinking about, and by now suppose
It is certainly not me.
But the crocus is up, and the lark, and the blundering
Blood knows what it knows.
It talks to itself all night, like a sliding moonlit sea.

Of course, it is talking of you.
At dawn, where the ocean has netted its catch of lights,
The sun plants one lithe foot
On that spill of mirrors, but the blood goes worming through
Its warm Arabian nights,
Naming your pounding name again in the dark heart-root.

Who shall, of course, be nameless.
Anyway, I should want you to know I have done my best,
As I'm sure you have, too.
Others are bound to us, the gentle and blameless
Whose names are not confessed
In the ceaseless palaver. My dearest, the clear unquarried blue

Of those depths is all but blinding.
You may remember that once you brought my boys
Two little woolly birds.
Yesterday the older one asked for you upon finding
Your thrush among his toys.
And the tides welled about me, and I could find no words.

There is not much else to tell.
One tries one's best to continue as before,
Doing some little good.
But I would have you know that all is not well
With a man dead set to ignore
The endless repetitions of his own murmurous blood.

THE SEVEN DEADLY SINS

Woodcuts by Leonard Baskin

PRIDE

"For me Almighty God Himself has died,"
Said one who formerly rebuked his pride
With, "Father, I am not worthy," and here denied
The Mercy by which each of us is tried.

ENVY

When, to a popular tune, God's Mercy and Justice
    Coagulate here again,
Establishing in tissue the True Republic
    Of good looks to all men
And victuals and wit and the holy sloth of the lily,
    Thou shalt not toil nor spin.

WRATH

I saw in stalls of pearl the heavenly hosts,
Gentle as down, and without private parts.
"Dies Irae," they sang, and I could smell
The dead-white phosphorus of sacred hearts.

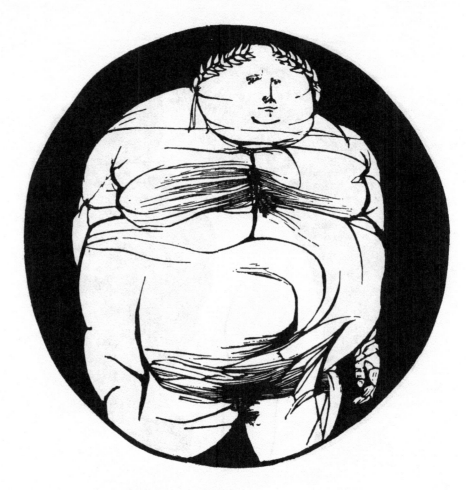

SLOTH

The first man leaps the ditch. (Who wins this race
     Wins laurel, but laurel dies.)
The next falls in (who in his hour of grace
     Plucked out his offending eyes).
The blind still lead. (Consider the ant's ways;
     Consider, and be wise.)

AVARICE

The penniless Indian fakirs and their camels
  Slip through the needle's eye
To bliss (for neither flesh nor spirit trammels
  Such as are prone to die)
And from emaciate heaven they behold
  Our sinful kings confer
Upon an infant huge tributes of gold
  And frankincense and myrrh.

GLUTTONY

Let the poor look to themselves, for it is said
Their savior wouldn't turn stones into bread.
And let the sow continually say grace.
For moss shall build in the lung and leave no trace,
The glutton worm shall tunnel in the head
And eat the Word out of the parchment face.

LUST

The Phoenix knows no lust, and Christ, our mother,
Suckles his children with his vintage blood.
Not to be such a One is to be other.

"MORE LIGHT! MORE LIGHT!"

for Heinrich Blücher and Hannah Arendt

Composed in the Tower before his execution
These moving verses, and being brought at that time
Painfully to the stake, submitted, declaring thus:
"I implore my God to witness that I have made no crime."

Nor was he forsaken of courage, but the death was horrible,
The sack of gunpowder failing to ignite.
His legs were blistered sticks on which the black sap
Bubbled and burst as he howled for the Kindly Light.

And that was but one, and by no means one of the worst;
Permitted at least his pitiful dignity;
And such as were by made prayers in the name of Christ,
That shall judge all men, for his soul's tranquillity.

We move now to outside a German wood.
Three men are there commanded to dig a hole
In which the two Jews are ordered to lie down
And be buried alive by the third, who is a Pole.

Not light from the shrine at Weimar beyond the hill
Nor light from heaven appeared. But he did refuse.
A Luger settled back deeply in its glove.
He was ordered to change places with the Jews.

Much casual death had drained away their souls.
The thick dirt mounted toward the quivering chin.
When only the head was exposed the order came
To dig him out again and to get back in.

No light, no light in the blue Polish eye.
When he finished a riding boot packed down the earth.
The Luger hovered lightly in its glove.
He was shot in the belly and in three hours bled to death.

No prayers or incense rose up in those hours
Which grew to be years, and every day came mute
Ghosts from the ovens, sifting through crisp air,
And settled upon his eyes in a black soot.

"IT OUT-HERODS HEROD. PRAY YOU, AVOID IT."

Tonight my children hunch
Toward their Western, and are glad
As, with a Sunday punch,
The Good casts out the Bad.

And in their fairy tales
The warty giant and witch
Get sealed in doorless jails
And the match-girl strikes it rich.

I've made myself a drink.
The giant and witch are set
To bust out of the clink
When my children have gone to bed.

All frequencies are loud
With signals of despair;
In flash and Morse they crowd
The rondure of the air.

For the wicked have grown strong,
Their numbers mock at death,
Their cow brings forth its young,
Their bull engendereth.

Their very fund of strength,
Satan, bestrides the globe;
He stalks its breadth and length
And finds out even Job.

Yet by quite other laws
My children make their case;
Half God, half Santa Claus,
But with my voice and face,

A hero comes to save
The poorman, beggarman, thief,
And make the world behave
And put an end to grief.

And that their sleep be sound
I say this Childermas
Who could not, at one time,
Have saved them from the gas.

from MILLIONS OF STRANGE
SHADOWS

THE COST

Why, let the stricken deer go weep,
The hart ungallèd play . . .

Think how some excellent, lean torso hugs
    The brink of weight and speed,
Coasting the margins of those rival tugs
    Down the thin path of friction,
The athlete's dancing vectors, the spirit's need,
    And muscle's cleanly diction,

Clean as a Calder, whose interlacing ribs
    Depend on one another,
Or a keen heeling of tackle, fluttering jibs
    And slotted centerboards,
A fleet of breasting gulls riding the smother
    And puzzle of heaven's wards.

Instinct with joy, a young Italian banks
    Smoothly around the base
Of Trajan's column, feeling between his flanks
    That cool, efficient beast,
His Vespa, at one with him in a centaur's race,
    Fresh from a Lapith feast,

And his Lapith girl behind him. Both of them lean
    With easy nonchalance
Over samphire-tufted cliffs which, though unseen,
    Are known, as the body knows
New risks and tilts, terrors and loves and wants,
    Deeply inside its clothes.

She grips the animal-shouldered naked skin
    Of his fitted leather jacket,
Letting a wake of hair float out the spin
    And dazzled rinse of air,
Yet for all their headlong lurch and flatulent racket
    They seem to loiter there,

Forever aslant in their moment and the mind's eye.
    Meanwhile, around the column
There also turn, and turn eternally,
    Two thousand raw recruits
And scarred veterans coiling the stone in solemn
    Military pursuits,

The heft and grit of the emperors' Dacian Wars
    That lasted fifteen years.
All of that youth and purpose is, of course,
    No more than so much dust.
And even Trajan, of his imperial peers
    Accounted "the most just,"

Honored by Dante, by Gregory the Great
    Saved from eternal Hell,
Swirls in the motes kicked up by the cough and spate
    Of the Vespa's blue exhaust,
And a voice whispers inwardly, "My soul,
    It is the cost, the cost,"

Like some unhinged Othello, who's just found out
    That justice is no more,
While Cassio, Desdemona, Iago shout
    Like true Venetians all,
"Go screw yourself; all's fair in love and war!"
    And the bright standards fall.

Better they should not hear that whispered phrase,
    The young Italian couple;
Surely the mind in all its brave assays
    Must put much thinking by,
To be, as Yeats would have it, free and supple
    As a long-legged fly.

Look at their slender purchase, how they list
        Like a blown clipper, brought
To the lively edge of peril, to the kissed
        Lip, the victor's crown,
The prize of life. Yet one unbodied thought
        Could topple them, bring down

The whole shebang. And why should they take thought
        Of all that ancient pain,
The Danube winters, the nameless young who fought,
        The blood's uncertain lease?
Or remember that that fifteen-year campaign
        Won seven years of peace?

BLACK BOY IN THE DARK

for Thomas Cornell

Peace, tawny slave, half me and half thy dam!
Did not thy hue bewray whose brat thou art, . . .
Villain, thou mightst have been an emperor.

Summer. A hot, moth-populated night.
Yesterday's maples in the village park
Are boxed away into the vaults of dark,
To be returned tomorrow, like our flag,
Which was brought down from its post office height
At sunset, folded, and dumped in a mailbag.

Wisdom, our Roman matron, perched on her throne
In front of the library, the Civil War
Memorial (History and Hope) no more
Are braced, trustworthy figures. Some witching skill
Softly dismantled them, stone by heavy stone,
And the small town, like Bethlehem, lies still.

And it is still at the all-night service station,
Where Andy Warhol's primary colors shine
In simple commercial glory, the Esso sign
Revolving like a funland lighthouse, where
An eighteen-year-old black boy clocks the nation,
Reading a comic book in a busted chair.

Our solitary guardian of the law
Of diminishing returns? The President,
Addressing the first contingent of draftees sent
To Vietnam, was brief: "Life is not fair,"
He said, and was right, of course. Everyone saw
What happened to him in Dallas. We were there,

We suffered, we were Whitman. And now the boy
Daydreams about the White House, the rising shares
Of Standard Oil, the whited sepulchres.
But what, after all, has he to complain about,
This expendable St. Michael we employ
To stay awake and keep the darkness out?

GREEN: AN EPISTLE

This urge, wrestle, resurrection of dry sticks,
Cut stems struggling to put down feet,
What saint strained so much,
Rose on such lopped limbs to a new life?
　　　　　　—THEODORE ROETHKE

     I write at last of the one forbidden topic
We, by a truce, have never touched upon:
Resentment, malice, hatred so inwrought
With moral inhibitions, so at odds with
The home-movie of yourself as patience, kindness,
And Charlton Heston playing Socrates,
That almost all of us were taken in,
Yourself not least, as to a giant Roxy,
Where the lights dimmed and the famous allegory
Of Good and Evil, clearly identified
By the unshaven surliness of the Bad Guys,
The virginal meekness of the ingénue,
Seduced us straight into that perfect world
Of Justice under God. Art for the sake
Of money, glamour, ego, self-deceit.
When we emerged into the assaulting sunlight,
We had a yen, like bad philosophers,
To go back to stay forever, there in the dark
With the trumpets, horses, and ancient Certitudes
On which, as we know, this great nation was founded,
Washington crossed the Delaware, and so forth.
And all of us, for an hour or so after,
Were Humphrey Bogart dating Ingrid Bergman,
Walking together but incommunicado
Till subway and homework knocked us out of it.
Yet even then, whatever we returned to
Was not, although we thought it was, the world.

I write at last on this topic because I am safe
Here in this grubby little border town
With its one cheap hotel. No one has my address.
The food is bad, the wine is too expensive,
And the local cathedral marred by restorations.
But from my balcony I view the east
For miles and, if I lean, the local sunsets
That bathe a marble duke with what must be
Surely the saddest light I have ever seen.
The air is thin and cool at this elevation,
And my desk wobbles unless propped with matchbooks.

It began, I suppose, as a color, yellow-green,
The tincture of spring willows, not so much color
As the sensation of color, haze that took shape
As a light scum, a doily of minutiae
On the smooth pool and surface of your mind.
A founding colony, Pilgrim amoebas
Descended from the gaseous flux when Zeus
Tossed down his great original thunderbolt
That flashed in darkness like an electric tree
Or the lit-up veins in an old arthritic hand.

Here is the microscope one had as a child,
The Christmas gift of some forgotten uncle.
Here is the slide with a drop of cider vinegar
As clear as gin, clear as your early mind.
Look down, being most careful not to see
Your own eye in the mirror underneath,
Which will appear, unless your view is right,
As a darkness on the face of the first waters.
When all is silvery and brilliant, look:
The long, thin, darting shapes, the flagellates,
Rat-tailed, ambitious, lash themselves along—
Those humble, floating ones, those simple cells
Content to be borne on whatever tide,
Trustful, the very image of consent—

These are the frail, unlikely origins,
Scarcely perceived, of all you shall become.
Scarcely perceived? But at this early age
(What are you, one or two?) you have no knowledge,
Nor do your folks, nor could the gravest doctors
Suspect that anything was really wrong.
Nor see the pale beginnings, lace endeavors
That with advancing ages shall mature
Into sea lettuce, beard the rocky shore
With a light green of soft and tidal hair.

     Whole eras, seemingly without event,
Now scud the glassy pool processionally
Until one day, misty, uncalendared,
As mild and unemphatic as a schwa,
Vascular tissue, conduit filaments
Learn how to feed the outposts of that small
Emerald principate. Now there are roots,
The filmy gills of toadstools, crested fern,
Quillworts, and foxtail mosses, and at last
Snapweed, loment, trillium, grass, herb Robert.
How soundlessly, shyly this came about,
One thinks today. But that is not the truth.
It was, from the first, an everlasting war
Conducted, as always, at gigantic cost.
Think of the droughts, the shifts of wind and weather,
The many seeds washed to some salt conclusion
Or brought to rest at last on barren ground.
Think of some inching tendrils worming down
In hope of water, blind and white as death.
Think of the strange mutations life requires.
Only the toughest endured, themselves much altered,
Trained in the cripple's careful sciences
Of mute accommodation. The survivors
Were all, one way or another, amputees
Who learned to live with their stumps, like Brueghel's beggars.

Yet, for all that, it clearly was a triumph,
Considering, as one must, what was to come.
And, even by themselves, those fields of clover,
Cattails, marsh bracken, water-lily pads
Stirred by the lightest airs, pliant, submissive—
Who could have called their slow creation *rage?*

Consider, as one must, what was to come.
Great towering conifers, deciduous,
Rib-vaulted elms, the banyan, oak, and palm,
Sequoia forests of vindictiveness
That also would go down on the death list
And, buried deep beneath alluvial shifts,
Would slowly darken into lakes of coal
And then under exquisite pressure turn
Into the tiny diamonds of pure hate.
The delicate fingers of the clematis
Feeling their way along a face of shale
With all the ingenuity of spite.
The indigestible thistle of revenge.
And your most late accomplishment, the rose.
Until at last, what we might designate
As your Third Day, behold a world of green:
Color of hope, of the Church's springtide vestments,
The primal wash, heraldic hue of envy.
But in what prelapsarian disguise!
Strangers and those who do not know you well
(Yourself not least) are quickly taken in
By a summery prospect, shades of innocence.
Like that young girl, a sort of chance acquaintance,
Seven or eight she was, on the New York Central,
Who, with a blue-eyed, beatific smile,
Shouted with joy, "Look, Mommy, quick. Look. Daisies!"

These days, with most of us at a safe distance,
You scarcely know yourself. Whole weeks go by
Without your remembering that enormous effort,
Ages of disappointment, the long ache
Of motives twisted out of recognition,
The doubt and hesitation all submerged
In those first clear waters, that untroubled pool.
Who could have hoped for this eventual peace?
Moreover, there are moments almost of bliss,
A sort of recompense, in which your mood
Sorts with the peach endowments of late sunlight
On a snowfield or on the breaker's froth
Or the white steeple of the local church.
Or, like a sunbather, whose lids retain
A greenish, gemmed impression of the sun
In lively, fluctuant geometries,
You sometimes contemplate a single image,
Utterly silent, utterly at rest.
It is of someone, a stranger, quite unknown,
Sitting alone in a foreign-looking room,
Gravely intent at a table propped with matchbooks,
Writing this very poem—about me.

SOMEBODY'S LIFE

I

Cliff-high, sunlit, in the tawny warmth of youth,
He gazed down at the breakneck rocks below,
Entranced by the water's loose attacks of jade,
The sousing waves, the interminable, blind
Fury of scattered opals, flung tiaras,
Full, hoisted, momentary chandeliers.
He spent most of the morning there alone.
He smoked, recalled some lines of poetry,
Felt himself claimed by such rash opulence:
These were the lofty figures of his soul.
What was it moved him in all that swash and polish?
Against an imperial sky of lupine blue,
Suspended, as it seemed to him, forever,
Blazed a sun-flooded gem of the first water.

II

Blazed, as it seemed, forever. Was this the secret
Gaudery of self-love, or a blood-bidden,
Involuntary homage to the world?
As it happens, he was doomed never to know.
At times in darkened rooms he thought he heard
The soft ruckus of patiently torn paper,
The sea's own noise, the elderly slop and suck
Of hopeless glottals. Once, in a bad dream,
He saw himself stranded on the wet flats,
As limp as kelp, among putrescent crabs.
But to the very finish he remembered
The flash and force, the crests, the heraldry,
Those casual epergnes towering up
Like Easter trinkets of the tzarevitch.

A BIRTHDAY POEM

June 22, 1976

Like a small cloud, like a little hovering ghost
　　　　Without substance or edges,
Like a crowd of numbered dots in a sick child's puzzle,
　　　　A loose community of midges
Sways in the carven shafts of noon that coast
Down through the summer trees in a golden dazzle.

Intent upon such tiny copter flights,
　　　　The eye adjusts its focus
To those billowings about ten feet away,
　　　　That hazy, woven hocus-pocus
Or shell game of the air, whose casual sleights
Leave us unable certainly to say

What lies behind it, or what sets it off
　　　　With fine diminishings,
Like the pale towns Mantegna chose to place
　　　　Beyond the thieves and King of Kings:
Those domes, theaters and temples, clear enough
On that mid-afternoon of our disgrace.

And we know at once it would take an act of will
　　　　Plus a firm, inquiring squint
To ignore those drunken motes and concentrate
　　　　On the blurred, unfathomed background tint
Of deep sea-green Holbein employed to fill
The space behind his ministers of state,

As if one range slyly obscured the other.
　　　　As, in the main, it does.
All of our Flemish distances disclose
　　　　A clarity that never was:
Dwarf pilgrims in the green faubourgs of Mother
And Son, stunted cathedrals, shrunken cows.

It's the same with Time. Looked at *sub specie*
     Aeternitatis, from
The snow-line of some Ararat of years,
     Scholars remark those kingdoms come
To nothing, to grief, without the least display
Of anything so underbred as tears,

And with their Zeiss binoculars descry
     Verduns and Waterloos,
The man-made mushroom's deathly overplus,
     Caesars and heretics and Jews
Gone down in blood, without batting an eye,
As if all history were deciduous.

It's when we come to shift the gears of tense
     That suddenly we note
A curious excitement of the heart
     And slight catch in the throat:—
When, for example, from the confluence
That bears all things away I set apart

The inexpressible lineaments of your face,
     Both as I know it now,
By heart, by sight, by reverent touch and study,
     And as it once was years ago,
Back in some inaccessible time and place,
Fixed in the vanished camera of somebody.

You are four years old here in this photograph.
     You are turned out in style,
In a pair of bright red sneakers, a birthday gift.
     You are looking down at them with a smile
Of pride and admiration, half
Wonder and half joy, at the right and the left.

The picture is black and white, mere light and shade.
                    Even the sneakers' red
Has washed away in acids. A voice is spent,
                    Echoing down the ages in my head:
What is your substance, whereof are you made,
That millions of strange shadows on you tend?

O my most dear, I know the live imprint
                    Of that smile of gratitude,
Know it more perfectly than any book.
                    It brims upon the world, a mood
Of love, a mode of gladness without stint.
O that I may be worthy of that look.

COMING HOME

from the journals of John Clare

They take away our belts so that we must hold
Our trousers up. The truly mad don't bother
And thus are oddly hobbled. Also our laces
So that our shoes do flop about our feet.
But I'm permitted exercise abroad
And feeling rather down and melancholy
Went for a forest walk. There I met gypsies
And sought their help to make good my escape
From the mad house. I confessed I had no money
But promised I should furnish them fifty pounds.
We fixed on Saturday. But when I returned
They had disappeared in their Egyptian way.
The sun set up its starlight in the trees
Which the breeze made to twinkle. They left behind
An old wide-awake hat on which I battened
As it might advantage me some later time.

JULY 20

Calmly, as though I purposed to converse
With the birds, as I am sometimes known to do,
I walked down the lane gently and was soon
In Enfield Town and then on the great York Road
Where it was all plain sailing, where no enemy
Displayed himself and I was without fear.
I made good progress, and by the dark of night
Skirted a marsh or pond and found a hovel
Floored with thick bales of clover and laid me down
As on the harvest of a summer field,
Companion to imaginary bees.
But I was troubled by uneasy dreams.
I thought my first wife lay in my left arm
And then somebody took her from my side
Which made me wake to hear someone say, "Mary,"
But nobody was by. I was alone.

I've made some progress, but being without food,
It is slower now, and I must void my shoes
Of pebbles fairly often, and rest myself.
I lay in a ditch to be out of the wind's way,
Fell into sleep for half an hour or so
And waked to find the left side of me soaked
With a foul scum and a soft mantling green.

* * *

I travel much at night, and I remember
Walking some miles under a brilliant sky
Almost dove-grey from closely hidden moonlight
Cast on the moisture of the atmosphere
Against which the tall trees on either side
Were unimaginably black and flat
And the puddles of the road flagstones of silver.

* * *

On the third day, stupid with weariness
And hunger, I assuaged my appetite
With eating grass, which seemed to taste like bread,
And seemed to do me good; and once, indeed,
It satisfied a king of Babylon.
I remember passing through the town of Buckden
And must have passed others as in a trance
For I recall none till I came to Stilton
Where my poor feet gave out. I found a tussock
Where I might rest myself, and as I lay down
I heard the voice of a young woman say,
"Poor creature," and another, older voice,
"He shams," but when I rose the latter said,
"O no he don't," as I limped quickly off.
I never saw those women, never looked back.

JULY 23

I was overtaken by a man and woman
Travelling by cart, and found them to be neighbors
From Helpstone where I used to live. They saw
My ragged state and gave me alms of fivepence
By which at the public house beside the bridge
I got some bread and cheese and two half-pints
And so was much refreshed, though scarcely able
To walk, my feet being now exceeding crippled
And I required to halt more frequently,
But greatly cheered at being in home's way.
I recognized the road to Peterborough
And all my hopes were up when there came toward me
A cart with a man, a woman and a boy.
When they were close, the woman leaped to the ground,
Seized both my hands and urged me toward the cart
But I refused and thought her either drunk
Or mad, but when I was told that she was Patty,
My second wife, I suffered myself to climb
Aboard and soon arrived at Northborough.
But Mary was not there. Neither could I discover
Anything of her more than the old story
That she was six years dead, intelligence
Of a doubtful newspaper some twelve years old;
But I would not be taken in by blarney
Having seen her very self with my two eyes
About twelve months ago, alive and young
And fresh and well and beautiful as ever.

"AUGURIES OF INNOCENCE"

A small, unsmiling child,
Held upon her shoulder,
Stares from a photograph
Slightly out of kilter.
It slipped from a loaded folder
Where the income tax was filed.
The light seems cut in half
By a glum, October filter.

Of course, the child is right.
The unleafed branches knot
Into hopeless riddles behind him
And the air is clearly cold.
Given the stinted light
To which fate and film consigned him,
Who'd smile at his own lot
Even at one year old?

And yet his mother smiles.
Is it grown-up make-believe,
As when anyone takes your picture,
Or some nobler, Roman virtue?
Vanity? Folly? The wiles
That some have up their sleeve?
A proud and flinty stricture
Against showing that things can hurt you,

Or a dark, Medean smile?
I'd be the last to know.
A speechless child of one
Could better construe the omens,
Unriddle our gifts for guile.
There's no sign from my son.
But it needs no Greeks or Romans
To foresee the ice and snow.

PERIPETEIA

Of course, the familiar rustling of programs,
My hair mussed from behind by a grand gesture
Of mink. A little craning about to see
If anyone I know is in the audience,
And, as the house fills up,
A mild relief that no one there knows me.
A certain amount of getting up and down
From my aisle seat to let the others in.
Then my eyes wander briefly over the cast,
Management, stand-ins, make-up men, designers,
Perfume and liquor ads, and rise prayerlike
To the false heaven of rosetted lights,
The stucco lyres and emblems of high art
That promise, with crude Broadway honesty,
Something less than perfection:
Two bulbs are missing and Apollo's bored.

And then the cool, drawn-out anticipation,
Not of the play itself, but the false dusk
And equally false night when the houselights
Obey some planetary rheostat
And bring a stillness on. It is that stillness
I wait for.
               Before it comes,
Whether we like it or not, we are a crowd,
Foul-breathed, gum-chewing, fat with arrogance,
Passion, opinion, and appetite for blood.
But in that instant, which the mind protracts,
From dim to dark before the curtain rises,
Each of us is miraculously alone
In calm, invulnerable isolation,
Neither a neighbor nor a fellow but,
As at the beginning and end, a single soul,
With all the sweet and sour of loneliness.
I, as a connoisseur of loneliness,
Savor it richly, and set it down
In an endless umber landscape, a stubble field

Under a lilac, electric, storm-flushed sky,
Where, in companionship with worthless stones,
Mica-flecked, or at best some rusty quartz,
I stood in childhood, waiting for things to mend.
A useful discipline, perhaps. One that might lead
To solitary, self-denying work
That issues in something harmless, like a poem,
Governed by laws that stand for other laws,
Both of which aim, through kindred disciplines,
At the soul's knowledge and habiliment.
In any case, in a self-granted freedom,
The mind, lone regent of itself, prolongs
The dark and silence; mirrors itself, delights
In consciousness of consciousness, alone,
Sufficient, nimble, touched with a small grace.

Then, as it must at last, the curtain rises,
The play begins. Something by Shakespeare.
Framed in the arched proscenium, it seems
A dream, neither better nor worse
Than whatever I shall dream after I rise
With hat and coat, go home to bed, and dream.
If anything, more limited, more strict—
No one will fly or turn into a moose.
But acceptable, like a dream, because remote,
And there is, after all, a pretty girl.
Perhaps tonight she'll figure in the cast
I summon to my slumber and control
In vast arenas, limitless space, and time
That yield and sway in soft Einsteinian tides.
Who is she? Sylvia? Amelia Earhart?
Some creature that appears and disappears
From life, from reverie, a fugitive of dreams?
There on the stage, with awkward grace, the actors,
Beautifully costumed in Renaissance brocade,
Perform their duties, even as I must mine,
Though not, as I am, always free to smile.

Something is happening. Some consternation.
Are the knives out? Is someone's life in danger?
And can the magic cloak and book protect?
One has, of course, real confidence in Shakespeare.
And I relax in my plush seat, convinced
That prompt as dawn and genuine as a toothache
The dream will be accomplished, provisionally true
As anything else one cares to think about.
The players are aghast. Can it be the villain,
The outrageous drunks, plotting the coup d'état,
Are slyer than we thought? Or we more innocent?
Can it be that poems lie? As in a dream,
Leaving a stunned and gap-mouthed Ferdinand,
Father and faery pageant, she, even she,
Miraculous Miranda, steps from the stage,
Moves up the aisle to my seat, where she stops,
Smiles gently, seriously, and takes my hand
And leads me out of the theater, into a night
As luminous as noon, more deeply real,
Simply because of her hand, than any dream
Shakespeare or I or anyone ever dreamed.

AFTER THE RAIN

for W. D. Snodgrass

The barbed-wire fences rust
As their cedar uprights blacken
After a night of rain.
Some early, innocent lust
Gets me outdoors to smell
The teasle, the pelted bracken,
The cold, mossed-over well,
Rank with its iron chain,

And takes me off for a stroll.
Wetness has taken over.
From drain and creeper twine
It's runnelled and trenched and edged
A pebbled serpentine
Secretly, as though pledged
To attain a difficult goal
And join some important river.

The air is a smear of ashes
With a cool taste of coins.
Stiff among misty washes,
The trees are as black as wicks,
Silent, detached and old.
A pallor undermines
Some damp and swollen sticks.
The woods are rich with mould.

How even and pure this light!
All things stand on their own,
Equal and shadowless,
In a world gone pale and neuter,
Yet riddled with fresh delight.
The heart of every stone
Conceals a toad, and the grass
Shines with a douse of pewter.

Somewhere a branch rustles
With the life of squirrels or birds,
Some life that is quick and right.
This queer, delicious bareness,
This plain, uniform light,
In which both elms and thistles,
Grass, boulders, even words,
Speak for a Spartan fairness,

Might, as I think it over,
Speak in a form of signs,
If only one could know
All of its hidden tricks,
Saying that I must go
With a cool taste of coins
To join some important river,
Some damp and swollen Styx.

Yet what puzzles me the most
Is my unwavering taste
For these dim, weathery ghosts,
And how, from the very first,
An early, innocent lust
Delighted in such wastes,
Sought with a reckless thirst
A light so pure and just.

THE FEAST OF STEPHEN

I

The coltish horseplay of the locker room,
Moist with the steam of the tiled shower stalls,
With shameless blends of civet, musk and sweat,
Loud with the cap-gun snapping of wet towels
Under the steel-ribbed cages of bare bulbs,
In some such setting of thick basement pipes
And janitorial realities
Boys for the first time frankly eye each other,
Inspect each other's bodies at close range,
And what they see is not so much another
As a strange, possible version of themselves,
And all the sparring dance, adrenal life,
Tense, jubilant nimbleness, is but a vague,
Busy, unfocussed ballet of self-love.

II

If the heart has its reasons, perhaps the body
Has its own lumbering sort of carnal spirit,
Felt in the tingling bruises of collision,
And known to captains as *esprit de corps.*
What is this brisk fraternity of timing,
Pivot and lobbing arc, or indirection,
Mens sana in men's sauna, in the flush
Of health and toilets, private and corporal glee,
These fleet caroms, *pliés* and genuflections
Before the salmon-leap, the leaping fountain
All sheathed in glistening light, flexed and alert?
From the vast echo-chamber of the gym,
Among the scumbled shouts and shrill of whistles,
The bounced basketball sound of a leather whip.

III

Think of those barren places where men gather
To act in the terrible name of rectitude,
Of acned shame, punk's pride, muscle or turf,
The bully's thin superiority.
Think of the *Sturm-Abteilungs Kommandant*
Who loves Beethoven and collects Degas,
Or the blond boys in jeans whose narrowed eyes
Are focussed by some hard and smothered lust,
Who lounge in a studied mimicry of ease,
Flick their live butts into the standing weeds,
And comb their hair in the mirror of cracked windows
Of an abandoned warehouse where they keep
In darkened readiness for their occasion
The rope, the chains, handcuffs and gasoline.

IV

Out in the rippled heat of a neighbor's field,
In the kilowatts of noon, they've got one cornered.
The bugs are jumping, and the burly youths
Strip to the waist for the hot work ahead.
They go to arm themselves at the dry-stone wall,
Having flung down their wet and salty garments
At the feet of a young man whose name is Saul.
He watches sharply these superbly tanned
Figures with a swimmer's chest and shoulders,
A miler's thighs, with their self-conscious grace,
And in between their sleek, converging bodies,
Brilliantly oiled and burnished by the sun,
He catches a brief glimpse of bloodied hair
And hears an unintelligible prayer.

THE ODDS

for Evan

Three new and matching loaves,
Each set upon a motionless swing seat,
Straight from some elemental stoves
And winter bakeries of unearthly wheat,
In diamonded, smooth pillowings of white
Have risen out of nothing overnight.

And all the woods for miles,
Stooped by these clean endowments of the north,
Flaunt the same candle-dripping styles
In poured combers of pumice and the froth
Of heady steins. Upon the railings lodge
The fat shapes of a nineteen-thirties Dodge.

Such perilous, toppling tides;
Such teeterings along uncertain perches.
A fragile cantilever hides
Even the chevrons of our veteran birches.
In this fierce hush there is a spell that heaves
Those huge arrested oceans in the eaves.

A sort of stagy show
Put on by a spoiled, eccentric millionaire.
Lacking the craft and choice that go
With weighed precision, meditated care,
Into a work of art, these are the spent,
Loose, aimless squanderings of the discontent.

Like the blind, headlong cells,
Crowding toward dreams of life, only to die
In dark fallopian canals,
Or that wild strew of bodies at My Lai.
Thick drifts, huddled embankments at our door
Pile up in this eleventh year of war.

Yet to these April snows,
This rashness, those incalculable odds,
    The costly and cold-blooded shows
Of blind perversity or spendthrift gods
My son is born, and in his mother's eyes
    Turns the whole war and winter into lies.

        But voices underground
Demand, "Who died for him? Who gave him place?"
    I have no answer. Vaguely stunned,
I turn away and look at my wife's face.
Outside the simple miracle of this birth
    The snowflakes lift and swivel to the earth

        As in those crystal balls
With Christmas storms of manageable size,
    A chalk precipitate that shawls
Antlers and roof and gifts beyond surmise,
A tiny settlement among those powers
    That shape our world, but that are never ours.

APPREHENSIONS

A grave and secret malady of my brother's,
The stock exchange, various grown-up shames,
The white emergency of hospitals,
Inquiries from the press, such *coups de théâtre*
Upon a stage from which I was excluded
Under the rubric of "benign neglect"
Had left me pretty much to my own devices
(My own stage was about seven years old)
Except for a Teutonic governess
Replete with the curious thumbprint of her race,
That special relish for inflicted pain.
Some of this she could vaguely satisfy
In the pages of the *Journal-American*
Which featured stories with lurid photographs—
A child chained tightly to a radiator
In an abandoned house; the instruments
With which some man tortured his fiancée;
A headless body recently unearthed
On the links of an exclusive country club—
That fleshed out terribly what loyal readers
Hankered for daily in the name of news.
(It in no way resembled the *New York Times,*
My parents' paper, thin on photographs.)
Its world, some half-lit world, some demi-monde,
I knew of only through Fräulein's addiction
To news that was largely terminal and obscene,
Winding its way between the ads for nightclubs
With girls wearing top hats, black tie, wing collar,
But without shirts, their naked breasts exposed;
And liquids that removed unsightly hair,
Treatments for corns, trusses and belts and braces.
She chain-smoked Camels as she scanned the pages,
Whereas my mother's brand was Chesterfield.

My primary education was composed
Of daily lessons in placating her
With acts of shameless, mute docility.
At seven I knew that I was not her equal,
If I knew nothing else. And I knew little,
But suspected a great deal—domestic quarrels,
Not altogether muffled, must have meant something.
"The market" of our home was the stock market,
Without visible fruit, without produce,
Except perhaps for the strange vendors of apples
Who filled our city streets. And all those girls—
The ones with naked breasts—there was some secret,
Deep as my brother's illness, behind their smiles.
They knew something I didn't; they taunted me.
I moved in a cloudy world of inference
Where the most solid object was a toy
Rake that my governess had used to beat me.

My own devices came to silence and cunning
In my unwilling exile, while attempting
To put two and two together, at which I failed.
The world seemed made of violent oppositions:
The Bull and Bear of Wall Street, Mother and Father,
Criminals and their victims, Venus and Mars,
The cold, portending graphics of the stars.
I spent my time in what these days my son
At three years old calls "grabbling around,"
For which Roget might possibly supply
"Purposeful idling, staying out of the way,"
Or, in the military phrase, "gold-bricking,"
A serious occupation, for which I was gifted
One Christmas with an all but magic treasure:
The Book of Knowledge, complete in twenty volumes.
I was its refugee, it was my Forest
Stocked with demure princesses, tameable dragons,
And sway-backed cottages, weighted with snow,
And waiting in an Arthur Rackham mist

For the high, secret advent of Santa Claus.
Dim populations of elfdom, and what's more,
Pictures of laborers in derby hats
And shirtsleeves, Thomas Alva Edison,
Who seemed to resemble Harding, who, in turn,
Resembled a kindly courtier, tactfully whispering
In the ear of Isabella, Queen of Spain—
Probably bearing on financial matters,
Selling the family jewels for Columbus,
Or whether the world is round. Serious topics
To which I would give due consideration.
There were puzzles and, magnificently, their answers;
Lively depictions of the Trojan War;
And Mrs. Siddons as The Tragic Muse.
Methods of calculating the height of trees,
Maps of the earth and heavens, buccaneer
Ventures for buried gold, and poetry:
Whittier, Longfellow, and "Home, Sweet Home."
Here was God's plenty, as Dryden said of Chaucer.

 Inestimable, priceless as that gift was,
I was given yet another—more peculiar,
Rare, unexpected, harder to assess,
An experience that W. H. Auden
Designates as "The Vision of Dame Kind,"
Remarking that "the objects of this vision
May be inorganic—mountains, rivers, seas,—
Or organic—trees and beasts—but they're non-human,
Though human artifacts may be included."

 We were living at this time in New York City
On the sixth floor of an apartment house
On Lexington, which still had streetcar tracks.
It was an afternoon in the late summer;
The windows open; wrought-iron window guards
Meant to keep pets and children from falling out.
I, at the window, studiously watching

A marvellous transformation of the sky;
A storm was coming up by dark gradations.
But what was curious about this was
That as the sky seemed to be taking on
An ashy blankness, behind which there lay
Tonalities of lilac and dusty rose
Tarnishing now to something more than dusk,
Crepuscular and funerary greys,
The streets became more luminous, the world
Glinted and shone with an uncanny freshness.
The brickwork of the house across the street
(A grim, run-down Victorian château)
Became distinct and legible; the air,
Full of excited imminence, stood still.
The streetcar tracks gleamed like the path of snails.
And all of this made me superbly happy,
But most of all a yellow Checker Cab
Parked at the corner. Something in the light
Was making this the yellowest thing on earth.
It was as if Adam, having completed
Naming the animals, had started in
On colors, and had found his primary pigment
Here, in a taxi cab, on Eighty-ninth Street.
It was the absolute, parental yellow.
Trash littered the gutter, the chipped paint
Of the lamppost still was chipped, but everything
Seemed meant to be as it was, seemed so designed,
As if the world had just then been created,
Not as a garden, but a rather soiled,
Loud, urban intersection, by God's will.
And then a chart of the Mississippi River,
With all her tributaries, flashed in the sky.
Thunder, beginning softly and far away,
Rolled down our avenue toward an explosion
That started with the sound of ripping cloth
And ended with a crash that made all crashes

Feeble, inadequate preliminaries.
And it began to rain. Someone or other
Called me away from there, and closed the window.

Reverberations (from the Latin, *verber*,
Meaning a whip or lash) rang down the alley
Of Lower Manhattan where George Washington
Stood in the cold, eying the ticker-tape,
Its latest bulletins getting worse and worse,
A ticking code of terminal messages.
The family jewels were gone. What had Columbus
(Who looked so noble in The Book of Knowledge)
Found for himself? Leg-irons. The Jersey flats.
More bodies than the *Journal-American*
Could well keep count of, most of them Indians.
And then one day there was discovered missing
My brother's bottle of phenobarbital—
And, as it later turned out, a razor blade.
How late in coming were all the revelations.
How dark and Cabbalistic the mysteries.
Messages all in cipher, enthymemes
Grossly suggestive, keeping their own counsel,
Vivid and unintelligible dreams.
A heartless regimen of exercises
Performed upon a sort of doorway gym
Was meant to strengthen my brother's hand and arm,
As hours with a stereopticon
His eyesight. But the doctor's tactful whispers
Were sibilant, Sibylline, inaudible.
There were, at last, when he returned to us,
My father's bandaged wrists. All the elisions
Cried loudly in a tongue I didn't know.
Finally, in the flat, declarative sentence
Of the encephalograph, the news was in:
In shocking lines the instrument described
My brother's malady as what the French,
Simply and full of awe, call *"le grand mal,"*
The Great Disease, Caesar's and Dostoyevsky's.

All of this seemed to prove, in a world where proof
Was often stinting, and the clues ominous,
That the *Journal-American* after all was right:
That sex was somehow wedded to disaster,
Pleasure and pain were necessary twins,
And that The Book of Knowledge and my vision
(Or whatever it was) were to be put away
With childish things, as, in the end, the world
As well as holy text insist upon.

    Just when it was that Fräulein disappeared
I don't recall. We continued to meet each other
By secret assignations in my dreams
In which, by stages, our relationship
Grew into international proportions
As the ghettos of Europe emptied, the box cars
Rolled toward enclosures terminal and obscene,
The ovens blazed away like Pittsburgh steel mills,
Chain-smoking through the night, and no one spoke.
We two would meet in a darkened living room
Between the lines of advancing allied troops
In the Wagnerian twilight of the *Reich.*
She would be seated by a table, reading
Under a lamp-shade of the finest parchment.
She would look up and say, "I always knew
That you would come to me, that you'd come home."
I would read over her shoulder, *"In der Heimat,
Im Heimatland, da gibts ein Wiedersehen."*
An old song of comparative innocence,
Until one learns to read between the lines.

THE GHOST IN THE MARTINI

Over the rim of the glass
Containing a good martini with a twist
I eye her bosom and consider a pass,
        Certain we'd not be missed

In the general hubbub.
Her lips, which I forgot to say, are superb,
Never stop babbling once (Aye, there's the rub)
        But who would want to curb

Such delicious, artful flattery?
It seems she adores my work, the distinguished grey
Of my hair. I muse on the salt and battery
        Of the sexual clinch, and say

Something terse and gruff
About the marked disparity in our ages.
She looks like twenty-three, though eager enough.
        As for the famous wages

Of sin, she can't have attained
Even to union scale, though you never can tell.
Her waist is slender and suggestively chained,
        And things are going well.

The martini does its job,
God bless it, seeping down to the dark old id.
("Is there no cradle, Sir, you would not rob?"
        Says ego, but the lid

Is off. The word is Strike
While the iron's hot.) And now, ingenuous and gay,
She is asking me about what I was like
        At twenty. (Twenty, eh?)

You wouldn't have liked me then,
I answer, looking carefully into her eyes.
I was shy, withdrawn, awkward, one of those men
    That girls seemed to despise,

    Moody and self-obsessed,
Unhappy, defiant, with guilty dreams galore,
Full of ill-natured pride, an unconfessed
    Snob and a thorough bore.

    Her smile is meant to convey
How changed or modest I am, I can't tell which,
When I suddenly hear someone close to me say,
    "You lousy son-of-a-bitch!"

    A young man's voice, by the sound,
Coming, it seems, from the twist in the martini.
"You arrogant, elderly letch, you broken-down
    Brother of Apeneck Sweeney!

    Thought I was buried for good
Under six thick feet of mindless self-regard?
Dance on my grave, would you, you galliard stud,
    Silenus in leotard?

    Well, summon me you did,
And I come unwillingly, like Samuel's ghost.
'All things shall be revealed that have been hid.'
    There's something for you to toast!

    You only got where you are
By standing upon my ectoplasmic shoulders,
And wherever that is may not be so high or far
    In the eyes of some beholders.

Take, for example, me.
I have sat alone in the dark, accomplishing little
And worth no more to myself, in pride and fee,
       Than a cup of lukewarm spittle.

      But honest about it, withal . . ."
("Withal," forsooth!) "Please not to interrupt.
And the lovelies went by, 'the long and the short and the tall,'
       Hankered for, but untupped.

      Bloody monastic it was.
A neurotic mixture of self-denial and fear;
The verse halting, the cataleptic pause,
       No sensible pain, no tear,

      But an interior drip
As from an ulcer, where, in the humid deep
Center of myself, I would scratch and grip
       The wet walls of the keep,

      Or lie on my back and smell
From the corners the sharp, ammoniac, urine stink.
'No light, but rather darkness visible.'
       And plenty of time to think.

      In that thick, fetid air
I talked to myself in giddy recitative:
'I have been studying how I may compare
       This prison where I live

      Unto the world . . .' I learned
Little, and was awarded no degrees.
Yet all that sunken hideousness earned
       Your negligence and ease.

Nor was it wholly sick,
Having procured you a certain modest fame;
A devotion, rather, a grim device to stick
    To something I could not name."

    Meanwhile, she babbles on
About men, or whatever, and the juniper juice
Shuts up at last, having sung, I trust, like a swan.
    Still given to self-abuse!

    Better get out of here;
If he opens his trap again it could get much worse.
I touch her elbow, and, leaning toward her ear,
    Tell her to find her purse.

"GLADNESS OF THE BEST"

for Hays Rockwell

Let us get up early to the vineyards; let us
see if the vine flourish, whether the tender
grape appear, and the pomegranates bud forth:
there will I give thee my loves.

See, see upon a field of royal blue,
Scaling the steep escarpments of the sky
      With gold-leafed curlicue,
Sepals and plumula and filigree,
      This vast, untrellised vine
Of scroll- and fretwork, a Jesse's family tree
Or ivy whose thick clamberings entwine
Heaven and earth and the viewer's raddling eye.

This mealed and sprinkled glittering, this park
Of "flowres delice" and Gobelin *millefleurs*
      Coiling upon the dark
In wild tourbillions, gerbs and golden falls
      Is a mere lace or grille
Before which Jesus works his miracles
Of love, feeding the poor, curing the ill,
Here in the Duc de Berry's *Très Riches Heures*;

And is itself the visible counterpart
Of fugal consort, branched polyphony,
      That dense, embroidered art
Of interleaved and deftly braided song
      In which each separate voice
Seems to discover where it should belong
Among its kind, and, fated by its choice,
Pursues a purpose at once fixed and free;

And every *cantus*, firm in its own pursuits,
Fluent and yet cast, as it were, in bronze,
      Exchanges brief salutes
And bows of courtesy at every turn

With every neighboring friend,
Bends to oblige each one with quick concern
And join them at a predetermined end
Of cordial and confirming antiphons.

Such music in its turn becomes the trope
Or figure of that holy amity
            Which is our only hope,
Enjoined upon us from two mountain heights:
            On Tables of The Law
Given at Sinai, and the Nazarite's
Luminous sermon that reduced to awe
And silence a vast crowd near Galilee.

Who could have known this better than St. George,
The Poet, in whose work these things are woven
            Or wrought as at a forge
Of disappointed hopes, of triumphs won
            Through strains of sound and soul
In that small country church at Bemerton?
This was the man who styled his ghostly role,
"Domestic servant to the King of Heaven."

If then, as in the counterpoises of
Music, the laity may bless the priest
            In an exchange of love,
Riposta for *Proposta*, all we inherit
            Returned and newly named
In the established words, "and with thy spirit,"
Be it with such clear grace as his who claimed,
Of all God's mercies, he was less than least.

from THE VENETIAN VESPERS

THE GRAPES

At five o'clock of a summer afternoon
We are already shadowed by the mountain
On whose lower slopes we perch, all of us here
At the *Hôtel de l'Univers et Déjeuner.*
The fruit trees and the stone lions out front
In deepening purple silhouette themselves
Against the bright green fields across the valley
Where, at the *Beau Rivage,* patrons are laved
In generous tides of gold. At cocktail time
Their glasses glint like gems, while we're eclipsed.
Which may explain
Why the younger set, which likes to get up late,
Assess its members over aperitifs,
Prefers that western slope, while we attract
A somewhat older, quieter clientele,
Americans mostly, though they seem to come
From everywhere, and are usually good tippers.
Still, it is strange and sad, at cocktail time,
To look across the valley from our shade,
As if from premature death, at all that brilliance
Across which silently on certain days
Shadows of clouds slide past in smooth parade,
While even our daisies and white irises
Are filled with blues and darkened premonitions.
Yet for our patrons, who are on holiday,
Questions of time are largely set aside.
They are indulgently amused to find
All the news magazines on the wicker table
In the lobby are outrageously outdated.
But Madame likes to keep them on display;
They add a touch of color, and a note
Of home and habit for many, and it's surprising
How thoroughly they are read on rainy days.
And I myself have smuggled one or two
Up to my bedroom, there to browse upon
Arrested time in *Time, Incorporated.*
There it is always 1954,

And Marlon Brando, perfectly preserved,
Sullen and brutal and desirable,
Avoids my eyes with a scowl; the record mile
Always belongs to Roger Bannister;
The rich and sleek of the international set
Are robbed of their furs and diamonds, get divorced
In a world so far removed from the rest of us
It almost seems arranged for our amusement
As they pose for pictures, perfectly made-up,
Coiffeured by Mr. Charles, languid, serene.
They never show up here—our little resort
Is far too mean for them—except in my daydreams.
My dreams at night are reserved for Marc-Antoine,
One of the bellboys at the *Beau Rivage*.
In his striped vest with flat buttons of brass
He comes to me every night after my prayers,
In fantasy, of course; in actual fact
He's taken no notice of me whatsoever.
Quite understandable, for I must be
Easily ten years older than he, and only
A chambermaid. As with all the very young,
To him the future's limitless and bright,
Anything's possible, one has but to wait.
No doubt it explains his native cheerfulness.
No doubt he dreams of a young millionairess,
Beautiful, spoiled and ardent, at his feet.
Perhaps it shall come to pass. Such things have happened.
Even barmaids and pantry girls have been seen
Translated into starlets tanning themselves
At the end of a diving board. But just this morning
Something came over me like the discovery
Of a deep secret of the universe.
It was early. I was in the dining room
Long before breakfast was served. I was alone.
Mornings, of course, it's we who get the light,
An especially tender light, hopeful and soft.
I stood beside a table near a window,

Gazing down at a crystal bowl of grapes
In ice-water. They were green grapes, or, rather,
They were a sort of pure, unblemished jade,
Like turbulent ocean water, with misted skins,
Their own pale, smoky sweat, or tiny frost.
I leaned over the table, letting the sun
Fall on my forearm, contemplating them.
Reflections of the water dodged and swam
In nervous incandescent filaments
Over my blouse and up along the ceiling.
And all those little bags of glassiness,
Those clustered planets, leaned their eastern cheeks
Into the sunlight, each one showing a soft
Meridian swelling where the thinning light
Mysteriously tapered into shadow,
To cool recesses, to the tranquil blues
That then were pillowing the *Beau Rivage*.
And watching I could almost see the light
Edge slowly over their simple surfaces,
And feel the sunlight moving on my skin
Like a warm glacier. And I seemed to know
In my blood the meaning of sidereal time
And know my little life had somehow crested.
There was nothing left for me now, nothing but years.
My destiny was cast and Marc-Antoine
Would not be called to play a part in it.
His passion, his Dark Queen, he'd meet elsewhere.
And I knew at last, with a faint, visceral twitch,
A flood of weakness that comes to the resigned,
What it must have felt like in that rubber boat
In mid-Pacific, to be the sole survivor
Of a crash, idly dandled on that blank
Untroubled waste, and see the light decline,
Taper and fade in graduated shades
Behind the International Date Line—
An accident I read about in *Time*.

THE DEODAND

What are these women up to? They've gone and strung
Drapes over the windows, cutting out light
And the slightest hope of a breeze here in mid-August.
Can this be simply to avoid being seen
By some prying *femme-de-chambre* across the boulevard
Who has stepped out on a balcony to disburse
Her dustmop gleanings on the summer air?
And what of these rugs and pillows, all haphazard,
Here in what might be someone's living room
In the swank, high-toned sixteenth *arrondissement?*
What would their fathers, husbands, fiancés,
Those pillars of the old *haute-bourgeoisie,*
Think of the strange charade now in the making?
Swathed in exotic finery, in loose silks,
Gauzy organzas with metallic threads,
Intricate Arab vests, brass ornaments
At wrist and ankle, those small sexual fetters,
Tight little silver chains, and bangled gold
Suspended like a coarse barbarian treasure
From soft earlobes pierced through symbolically,
They are preparing some *tableau vivant.*
One girl, consulting the authority
Of a painting, perhaps by Ingres or Delacroix,
Is reporting over her shoulder on the use
Of kohl to lend its dark, savage allurements.
Another, playing the slave-artisan's role,
Almost completely naked, brush in hand,
Attends to these instructions as she prepares
To complete the seductive shadowing of the eyes
Of the blonde girl who appears the harem favorite,
And who is now admiring these effects
In a mirror held by a fourth, a well-clad servant.
The scene simmers with Paris and women in heat,
Darkened and airless, perhaps with a faint hum

Of trapped flies, and a strong odor of musk.
For whom do they play at this hot indolence
And languorous vassalage? They are alone
With fantasies of jasmine and brass lamps,
Melons and dates and bowls of rose-water,
A courtyard fountain's firework blaze of prisms,
Its basin sown with stars and *poissons d'or,*
And a rude stable smell of animal strength,
Of leather thongs, hinting of violations,
Swooning lubricities and lassitudes.
What is all this but crude imperial pride,
Feminized, scented and attenuated,
The exploitation of the primitive,
Homages of romantic self-deception,
Mimes of submission glamorized as lust?
Have they no intimation, no recall
Of the once queen who liked to play at milkmaid,
And the fierce butcher-reckoning that followed
Her innocent, unthinking masquerade?
Those who will not be taught by history
Have as their curse the office to repeat it,
And for this little spiritual debauch
(Reported here with warm, exacting care
By Pierre Renoir in 1872—
Apparently unnoticed by the girls,
An invisible voyeur, like you and me)
Exactions shall be made, an expiation,
A forfeiture. Though it take ninety years,
All the retributive iron of Racine
Shall answer from the raging heat of the desert.

In the final months of the Algerian war
They captured a very young French Legionnaire.
They shaved his head, decked him in a blonde wig,
Carmined his lips grotesquely, fitted him out
With long, theatrical false eyelashes
And a bright, loose-fitting skirt of calico,

And cut off all the fingers of both hands.
He had to eat from a fork held by his captors.
Thus costumed, he was taken from town to town,
Encampment to encampment, on a leash,
And forced to beg for his food with a special verse
Sung to a popular show tune of those days:
"Donnez moi à manger de vos mains
Car c'est pour vous que je fais ma petite danse;
Car je suis Madeleine, la putain,
Et je m'en vais le lendemain matin,
Car je suis La Belle France."

THE SHORT END

Here the anthem doth commence:
Love and Constancy is dead,
Phoenix and the turtle fled
In a mutual flame from hence.

I

"Greetings from Tijuana!" on a ground
Of ripe banana rayon with a fat
And couchant Mexican in mid-siesta,
Wrapped in a many-colored Jacobin
Serape, and more deeply rapt in sleep,
Head propped against a phallic organ cactus
Of shamrock green, all thrown against a throw
Of purple on a Biedermeier couch—
This is the latest prize, newly unwrapped,
A bright and shiny capstone to the largest
Assemblage of such pillows in the East:
Pillows from Kennebunkport, balsam-scented
And stuffed with wood chips, pillows from Coney Island
Blazoned with Ferris Wheels and Roller Coasters,
Pillows that fart when sat on, tasselled pillows
From Old New Orleans, creole and redly carnal,
And what may be the gem of the collection,
From the New York World's Fair of Thirty-Nine,
Bearing a white Trylon and Perisphere,
Moderne, severe and thrilling, on the recto;
And on the verso in gold and blue italics
The Fair's motto: "A Century of Progress."
To this exciting find, picked up for pennies
At a garage sale in Schenectady
(Though slightly soiled with ketchup at one corner)
Yosemite, Niagara, Honolulu
Have yielded place, meekly accepting exile
In the mud room, the conversation pit,
Or other unpeopled but bepillowed rooms.
This far-flung empire, these domains belong
To Shirley Carson and her husband, "Kit,"
Softening the hard edges of their lives.

Shirley is curator, museum guide,
The Mellon and the Berenson of these
Mute instances (except for the hidden farts)
Of fustian and of bombast, crocheted, embroidered
And stencilled with bright Day-Glo coloring.
They cheer her with their brilliance, with their sleek
And travelled worldliness, and serve as cover,
In the literal sense, a plumped and bolstered cover,
For the booze she needs to have always at hand.
There used to be a game, long since abandoned,
In which he'd try to find what she concealed.
"Cooler," she'd say, "yer gettin' really icy,"
She'd say, "so whyantcha fix yerself a drink?"
As he sought vainly behind Acapulco,
All flame and orange satin, or underneath
A petit point of moviedom's nobility:
A famous, genuine Hollywood Marquee,
Below which stood a spurious Romanov.
He quit because she always had reserves,
What she called "liquid assets," tucked away.
He had tried everything over the years.
There was no appealing to her vanity;
She was now puffily fat and pillowy.
Reason, of course, was futile, and he'd learned
That strong-arm methods strengthened her defiance.
These days he came home from the body shop
He owned and operated, its walls thumb-tacked
With centerfolded bodies from *Playboy*,
Yielding, expectant, invitational,
Came home oil-stained and late to find her drunk
And the house rank with the staleness of dead butts.
Staleness, that's what it was, he used to say
To himself, trying to figure what went wrong,
Emptying ashtrays of their ghostly wreckage,
Their powders and cremations of the past.
He always went to bed long before she did.
She would sit up till late, smoking and drinking,

Afloat upon a wild surfeit of colors,
The midway braveries, harlequin streamers,
Or skewbald, carney liveries of the macaw,
Through which, from time to time, memories arose.

II

Of these, two were persistent. In one of them
She was back in the first, untainted months of marriage,
Slight, shy, and dressed in soft ecru charmeuse,
Hopeful, adoring, and in return adored
By her husband, who was then a travelling salesman.
The company had scheduled a convention
In Atlantic City, and had generously
Invited the men to bring along their wives.
They were to stay in triumph at the Marlborough-
Blenheim, a luxury resort hotel
That ran both fresh and salt water in its tubs,
And boasted an international string ensemble
That assembled every afternoon at four
For *thé dansant*, when the very air was rich
With Jerome Kern, Romberg, and Rudolf Friml.
The room they were assigned gave on an air shaft
But even so they could smell the black Atlantic,
And being hidden away, she told herself,
Was just the thing for newlyweds, and made
Forays on the interminable vista
Of the boardwalk—it seemed to stretch away
In hazy diminution, like the prospects
Or boxwood avenues of a château—
The more exciting. Or so it seemed in prospect.
She recalled the opulent soft wind-chime music,
A mingling of silverware and ice-water
At their first breakfast in the dining room.
Also another sound. That of men's voices
Just slightly louder than was necessary
For the tablemates they seemed to be addressing.

It bore some message, all that baritone
Brio of masculine snort and self-assertion.
It belonged with cigars and bets and locker rooms.
It had nothing to do with damask and chandeliers.
It was a sign, she knew at once, of something.
They wore her husband's same convention badge,
So must be salesmen, here for a pep talk
And booster from top-level management,
Young, hopeful, energetic, just like him,
But, in some way she found unnerving, louder.
That was the earliest omen.
                                        The second was
The vast boardwalk itself, its herringbone
Of seasoned lumber lined on the inland side
By Frozen Custard booths, Salt Water Taffy
Kneaded and stretched by large industrial cams,
Pinball and shooting galleries with Kewpie Dolls,
Pink dachshunds, cross-eyed ostriches for prizes,
Fun Houses, Bumpum Cars and bowling alleys,
And shops that offered the discriminating
Hand-decorated shells, fantastic landscapes
Entirely composed of varnished starfish,
And other shops displaying what was called
"Sophisticated Nightwear For My Lady,"
With black-lace panties bearing a crimson heart
At what might be Mons Veneris' timberline,
Flesh-toned brassieres with large rose-window cutouts
Edged with elaborate guimpe, rococo portholes
Allowing the nipples to assert themselves,
And see-through nightgowns bordered with angora
Or frowsy feather boas of magenta.
Here she was free to take the healthful airs,
Inhale the unclippered trade-winds of New Jersey
And otherwise romp and disport herself
From nine until five-thirty, when her husband,
Her only Norman, would be returned to her.
Such was this place, a hapless rural seat

And sandy edge of the Truck Garden State,
The dubious North American Paradise.

III

It was just after dinner their second evening
That a fellow-conventioneer, met in the lobby,
Invited them to join a little party
For a libation in the Plantagenet Bar
And Tap Room; he performed the introductions
To Madge and Felix, Bubbles and Billy Jim,
Astrid, and lastly, to himself, Maurice,
Whose nickname, it appeared, was Two Potato,
And things were on a genial, first-name basis
Right from the start, so it was only after
The second round of drinks (which both the Carsons
Intended as their last, and a sufficient
Fling at impromptu sociability)
That it was inadvertently discovered
That the Carsons were little more than newlyweds
On what amounted to their honeymoon.
No one would hear of them leaving, or trying to pay
For anything. Another round of drinks
Was ordered. Two Potato proclaimed himself
Their host, and winked at them emphatically.
There followed much raucous, suggestive toasting,
Norman was designated "a stripling kid,"
And ceremoniously nicknamed "Kit,"
And people started calling Shirley "Shirl,"
And "Curly-Shirl" and "Shirl-Girl." There were displays
Of mock-tenderness toward the young couple
And gags about the missionary position,
With weak, off-key, off-color attempts at singing
"Rock of Ages," with hands clasped in prayer
And eyes raised ceilingward at "cleft for me,"
Eyes closed at "let me hide myself in thee,"
The whole number grotesquely harmonized

In the manner of a barbershop quartet.
By now she wanted desperately to leave
But couldn't figure out the way to do so
Without giving offense, seeming ungrateful;
And somehow, she suspected, they knew this.
Two Potato particularly seemed
Aggressive both in his solicitude
And in the smirking lewdness of his jokes
As he unblushingly eyed the bride for blushes
And gallantly declared her "a good sport,"
"A regular fella," and "the little woman."
She knew when the next round of drinks appeared
That she and Norman were mere hostages
Whom nobody would ransom. Billy Jim asked
If either of them knew a folk-song called
"The Old Gism Trail," and everybody laughed,
Laughed at the plain vulgarity itself
And at the Carsons' manifest discomfort
And at their pained, inept attempt at laughter.
The merriment was acid and complex.
Felix it was who kept proposing toasts
To "good ol' Shirl an' Kit," names which he slurred
Both in pronunciation and disparagement
With an expansive, wanton drunkenness
That in its license seemed soberly planned
To increase by graduated steps until
Without seeming aware of what he was doing
He'd raise a toast to "good ol' Curl an' Shit."
They managed to get away before that happened,
Though Shirley knew in her bones it was intended,
Had seen it coming from a mile away.
They left, but not before it was made clear
That they were the only married couple present,
That the other men had left their wives at home,
And that this was what conventions were all about.
The Carsons were made to feel laughably foolish,
Timid and prepubescent and repressed,

And with a final flourish of raised glasses
The "guests" were at last permitted to withdraw.

IV

   Fade-out; assisted by a dram of gin,
And a soft radio soundtrack bringing up
A velvety chanteur who wants a kiss
By wire, in some access of chastity,
Yet in a throaty passion volunteers,
"Baby, mah heart's on fire." Fade-in with pan
Shot of a highway somewhere south of Wheeling
Where she and her husband, whom she now calls Kit,
Were driving through a late day in November
Toward some goal obscure as the very weather,
Defunctive, moist, overcast, requiescent.
Rounding a bend, they came in sudden view
Of what seemed a caravan of trucks and cars,
A long civilian convoy, parked along
The right-hand shoulder, and instantly slowed down,
Fearing a speed-trap or an accident.
It was instead, as a billboard announced,
A LIVE ENTOMBMENT—CONTRIBUTIONS PLEASE.
They found a parking slot, directed by
Two courteous State Troopers with leather holsters
That seemed tumescent with heavy, flopping side-arms,
And made their way across the stony ground
To a strange, silent crowd, as at a graveside.
A poster fixed to a tree gave the details:
"Here lies George Rose in a casket supplied by
The Memento Morey Funeral Home of Wheeling.
He has been underground 38 days.
[The place for the numbers was plastered with new stickers.]
He lives on liquids and almond Hershey bars
Fed through the speaking tube next to his head,
By which his brother and custodian,
John Wesley Rose, communicates with him,

And by means of which he breathes. Note that the tube
Can be bent sideways to keep out the rain.
Visitors are invited to put all questions
To the custodian because George Rose
Is eager to preserve his solitude.
He has forsworn the vanities of this world.
Donations will be gratefully accepted."
At length she wedged her way among the curious
To where she saw a varnished pinewood box
With neatly mitred corners, fitted with glass
At the top, and measuring roughly a foot square,
Sunk in the earth, protruding about three inches.
Through this plain aperture she now beheld
The pale, expressionless features of George Rose,
Bearded, but with a pocked, pitted complexion,
And pale blue eyes conveying by their blankness
A boredom so profound it might indeed
Pass for a certain otherworldliness,
Making it eminently clear to all
That not a single face that showed itself
Against the sky for his consideration
Was found by him to be beautiful or wise
Or worthy of the least notice or interest.
One could tell he was alive because he blinked.
At the crowd's edge, near the collection box,
Stood a man who was almost certainly his brother,
Caretaker and custodian, engaged
In earnest talk with one of the State Troopers.
It crossed her mind to wonder how they dealt
With his evacuations, yet she couldn't
Ask such a question of an unknown man.
But Kit seemed to have questions of his own
And as he approached John Wesley she turned away
To the edge of a large field and stood alone
In some strange wordless seizure of distress.
She turned her gaze deliberately away
From the road, the cars, the little clustered knot

Of humankind around that sheet of glass,
Like flies around a dish of sweetened water,
And focussed intently on what lay before her.
A grizzled landscape, burdock and thistle-choked,
A snarled, barbed-wire barricade of brambles,
All thorn and needle-sharp hostility.
The dead weeds wicker-brittle, raffia-pale,
The curled oak leaves a deep tobacco brown,
The sad rouge of old bricks, chips of cement
From broken masonry, a stubble field
Like a mangy lion's pelt of withered grass.
Off in the distance a thoroughly dead tree,
Peeled of its bark, sapless, an armature
Of well-groomed, military silver-grey.
And other leafless trees, their smallest twigs
Incising a sky the color of a bruise.
In all the rancid, tannic, mustard tones,
Mud colors, lignum greys and mottled rocks,
The only visible relief she found
Was the plush red velvet of the sumac spikes
And the slick, vinyl, Stygian, anthracite
Blackness of water in a drainage ditch.
The air sang with the cold of empty caves,
Of mildew, cobwebs, slug and maggot life.
And at her feet, among the scattered stubs
Of water-logged non-filter cigarettes,
Lay a limp length of trampled fennel stalk.
And then she heard, astonishingly close,
Right at her side, the incontestable voice
Of someone who could not possibly be there:
Of old Miss McIntosh, her eleventh grade
Latin instructor, now many years dead,
Saying with slow, measured authority,
"It is your duty to remain right here.
Those people and their cars will go away.
Norman will go. George Rose will stay where he is,
But you have nothing whatever to do with him.

He will die quietly inside his coffin.
From time to time you will be given water
And a peanut butter sandwich on white bread.
You will stay here as long as it shall take
To love this place so much you elect to stay
Forever, forsaking all others you have known
Or dreamed of or incontinently longed for.
Look at and meditate upon the crows.
Think upon God. Humbly prepare yourself,
Like the wise virgins in the parable,
For the coming resurrection of George Rose.
Consider deeply why as the first example
Of the first conjugation—which is not
As conjugal as some suppose—one learns
The model verb forms of 'to love,' *amare*,
Which also happens to be the word for 'bitter.'
Both love and Latin are more difficult
Than is usually imagined or admitted.
This is your final exam; this is your classroom."

                    V

    Another voice drowns out Miss McIntosh.
It's Mel Tormé, singing "Who's Sorry Now?"
Followed by a Kid Ory version of
"Quincy Street Stomp," and bringing back in view
The bright upholstery of the present tense,
The lax geography of pillows, gin-
And-bitters with anesthetic bitterness.
It must be three a.m., but never mind.
Open upon her lap lies *The New Yorker*,
Exhibiting a full-page color ad
For the Scotch whiskey-based liqueur, Drambuie,
Soft-focus, in the palest tints of dawn.
Therein a lady and a gentleman
Stand gazing north from the triumphal arch
That Stanford White designed for Washington Square.

She wears an evening gown of shocking pink
And a mink stole. Her escort, in black tie,
Standing behind her, his arms about her waist,
Follows her gaze uptown where a peach haze
Is about to infuse the windows of the rich.
Meanwhile, this couple, who have just descended
From a hansom cab departing toward the east,
Have all Fifth Avenue stretched out before them
In Élysée prospectus, like the calm fields
Where Attic heroes dwell. They are alone
On the blank street. The truths of economics,
The dismal (decimal) science, dissolve away
In the faint light, and leave her standing there,
Shirley herself, suddenly slim again,
In the arms of a young nameless gentleman.
To be sure, the salmon hues up in the Eighties,
Flushing the Metropolitan's facade,
Glinting on silver tops of skyscrapers
As upon factory-made, hand-polished Alps
(Though the deep canyons still repose in darkness)
Bespeak the calm beneficence of dawn
When they shall both raise up their brandy glasses
Filled with that admirable Scotch liqueur
Or else with gin and tolerable bitters
And toast each other in some nearby penthouse.
But meanwhile her attention is wholly drawn
To the carriage lantern on the hansom cab.
A kerosene lantern with a concave shield
Or chrome reflector inside a box of glass.
The quivering flame of the broad ribbon wick
Itself presents a quick array of colors,
All brilliance, light, intensity and hope.
The flames flow upward from a rounded base
Like an inverted waterfall of gold,
Yet somehow at the center, the pure kernel
Of fire is pearly, incandescent white.
Out of that whiteness all the celestial hues

Of dawn proliferate in wobbly spectra,
Lilac and orange, the rust of marigold,
The warm and tropic colors of the world
That she inhabits, that she has collected
And stuffed like assorted trophies of the kill.
The shape of flames is almond-like, the shape
Of Egyptian eyes turned sideways, garlic cloves,
Camel-hair tips of watercolor brushes,
Of waterdrops. The shape performs a dance,
A sinuous, erotic wavering,
All inference and instability,
Shimmy and glitter. It is, she suddenly knows,
The figure *redivivus* of George Rose,
Arisen, youthful, strong and roseate,
Tiny, of course, pathetically reduced
To pinky size, but performing a lewd dance
Of Shiva, the rippling muscles of his thighs
And abdomen as fluent as a river
Of upward-pouring color, the golden finish
Of Sardanapalus, emphatic rhythms
Of blues and body language, a centrifuge
Of climbing braids that beautifully enlarge,
Thicken and hang pendulous in the air.
Out of these twinings, foldings, envelopings
Of brass and apricot, biceps and groin,
She sees the last thing she will ever see:
The purest red there is, passional red,
Fire-engine red, the red of Valentines,
Of which she is herself the howling center.

STILL LIFE

Sleep-walking vapor, like a visitant ghost,
      Hovers above a lake
Of Tennysonian calm just before dawn.
Inverted trees and boulders waver and coast
In polished darkness. Glints of silver break
Among the liquid leafage, and then are gone.

Everything's doused and diamonded with wet.
      A cobweb, woven taut
On bending stanchion frames of tentpole grass,
Sags like a trampoline or firemen's net
With all the glitter and riches it has caught,
Each drop a paperweight of Steuben glass.

No birdsong yet, no cricket, nor does the trout
      Explode in water-scrolls
For a skimming fly. All that is yet to come.
Things are as still and motionless throughout
The universe as ancient Chinese bowls,
And nature is magnificently dumb.

Why does this so much stir me, like a code
      Or muffled intimation
Of purposes and preordained events?
It knows me, and I recognize its mode
Of cautionary, spring-tight hesitation,
This silence so impacted and intense.

As in a water-surface I behold
      The first, soft, peach decree
Of light, its pale, inaudible commands.
I stand beneath a pine-tree in the cold,
Just before dawn, somewhere in Germany,
A cold, wet Garand rifle in my hands.

PERSISTENCES

The leafless trees are feathery,
   A foxed, Victorian lace,
Against a sky of milk-glass blue,
   Blank, washed-out, commonplace.

Between them and my window
   Huge helices of snow
Perform their savage, churning rites
   At seventeen below.

The obscurity resembles
   A silken Chinese mist
Wherein through calligraphic daubs
   Of artistry persist

Pocked and volcanic gorges,
   Clenched and arthritic pines,
Faint, coral-tinted herons' legs
   Splashing among the tines

Of waving, tasselled marshgrass,
   Deep pools aflash with sharp,
Shingled and burnished armor-plate
   Of sacred, child-eyed carp.

This dimness is dynastic,
   An ashen T'ang of age
Or blur that grudgingly reveals
   A ghostly equipage,

Ancestral deputations
   Wound in the whited air,
To whom some sentry flings a slight,
   Prescriptive, "Who goes there?"

Are these the apparitions
    Of enemies or friends?
Loved ones from whom I once withheld
    Kindnesses or amends

On preterite occasions
    Now lost beyond repeal?
Or the old childhood torturers
    Of undiminished zeal,

Adults who ridiculed me,
    Schoolmates who broke my nose,
Risen from black, unconscious depths
    Of REM repose?

Who comes here seeking justice,
    Or in its high despite,
Bent on some hopeless interview
    On wrongs nothing can right?

Those throngs disdain to answer,
    Though numberless as flakes;
Mine is the task to find out words
    For their memorial sakes

Who press in dense approaches,
    Blue numeral tattoos
Writ crosswise on their arteries,
    The burning, voiceless Jews.

THE VENETIAN VESPERS

for Harry and Kathleen Ford

. . . where's that palace whereinto foul things
Sometimes intrude not? Who has a breast so pure
But some uncleanly apprehensions
Keep leets and law days, and in session sit
With meditations lawful?
                    —*Othello*: III, iii, 136–41

We cannot all have our gardens now, nor our pleasant fields to
meditate in at eventide.
        —RUSKIN: *The Stones of Venice*, BK. I, CH. XXX

I

What's merciful is not knowing where you are,
What time it is, even your name or age,
But merely a clean coolness at the temple—
That, says the spirit softly, is enough
For the mind to adventure on its half-hidden path
Like starlight interrupted by dense trees
Journeying backwards on a winter trip
While you are going, as you fancy, forward,
And the stars are keeping pace with everything.
Where to begin? With the white, wrinkled membrane,
The disgusting skin that gathers on hot milk?
Or narrow slabs of jasper light at sundown
That fit themselves softly around the legs
Of chairs, and entertain a drift of motes,
A tide of sadness, a failing, a dying fall?
Or the glass jar, like a wet cell battery,
Full of electric coils and boiling resins,
Its tin Pinocchio nose with one small nostril,
And both of us under a tent of towels
Like child conspirators, the tin nose breathing
Health at me steadily, like the insufflation of God?
Yes, but also the sight, on a grey morning,
Beneath the crossbar of an iron railing

Painted a glossy black, of six waterdrops
Slung in suspension, sucking into themselves,
As if it were some morbid nourishment,
The sagging blackness of the rail itself,
But edged with brilliant fingernails of chrome
In which the world was wonderfully disfigured
Like faces seen in spoons, like mirrorings
In the fine spawn, the roe of air bubbles,
That tiny silver wampum along the stems,
Yellowed and magnified, of aging flowers
Caught in the lens of stale water and glass
In the upstairs room when somebody had died.
Just like the beads they sprinkled over cookies
At Christmas. Or perhaps those secret faces
Known to no one but me, slyly revealed
In repetitions of the wallpaper,
My tight network of agents in the field.
Well, yes. Any of these might somehow serve
As a departure point. But, perhaps, best
Would be those first precocious hints of hell,
Those intuitions of living desolation
That last a lifetime. These were never, for me,
Some desert place that humans had avoided
In which I could get lost, to which I might
In dreams condemn myself—a wilderness
Natural but alien and unpitying.
They were instead those derelict waste places
Abandoned by mankind as of no worth,
Frequented, if at all, by the dispossessed,
Nocturnal shapes, the crippled and the shamed.
Here in the haywire weeds, concealed by wilds
Of goldenrod and toadflax, lies a spur
With its one boxcar of brick-colored armor,
At noon, midsummer, fiercer than a kiln,
Rippling the thinness of the air around it
With visible distortions. Among the stones
Of the railbed, fragments of shattered amber

That held a pint of rye. The carapace
Of a dried beetle. A broken orange crate
Streaked with tobacco stains at the nailheads
In the grey, fractured slats. And over all
The dust of oblivion finer than milled flour
Where chips of brick, clinkers and old iron
Burn in their slow, invisible decay.
Or else it is late afternoon in autumn,
The sunlight rusting on the western fronts
Of a long block of Victorian brick houses,
Untenanted, presumably condemned,
Their brownstone grapes, their grand entablatures,
Their straining caryatid muscle-men
Rendered at once ridiculous and sad
By the black scars of zigzag fire escapes
That double themselves in isometric shadows.
And all their vacancy is given voice
By the endless flapping of one window-shade.
And then there is the rank, familiar smell
Of underpasses, the dark piers of bridges,
Where old men, the incontinent, urinate.
The acid smell of poverty, the jest
Of adolescent boys exchanging quips
About bedpans, the motorman's comfort,
A hospital world of syphons and thick tubes
That they know nothing of. Nor do they know
The heatless burnings of the elderly
In memorized, imaginary lusts,
Visions of noontide infidelities,
Crude hallway gropings, cruel lubricities,
A fire as cold and slow as rusting metal.
It's but a child's step, it's but an old man's totter
From this to the appalling world of dreams.
Grey bottled babies in formaldehyde
As in their primal amniotic bath.
Pale dowagers hiding their liver-spots
In a fine chalk, confectionery dust.

And then the unbearable close-up of a wart
With a tough bristle of hair, like a small beast
With head and feet tucked under, playing possum.
A meat-hooked ham, hung like a traitor's head
For the public's notice in a butcher shop,
Faintly resembling the gartered thigh
Of an acrobatic, overweight soubrette.
And a scaled, crusted animal whose head
Fits in a Nazi helmet, whose webbed feet
Are cold on the white flanks of dreaming lovers,
While thorned and furry legs embrace each other
As black mandibles tick. Immature girls,
Naked but for the stockings they stretch tight
To tempt the mucid glitter of an eye.
And the truncated snout of a small bat,
Like one whose nose, undermined by the pox,
Falls back to the skull's socket. Deepest of all,
Like the converging lines in diagrams
Of vanishing points, those underwater blades,
Those quills or sunburst spokes of marine light,
Flutings and gilded shafts in which one sees
In the drowned star of intersecting beams
Just at that final moment of suffocation
The terrifying and unmeaning rictus
Of the sandshark's stretched, involuntary grin.
In the upstairs room, when somebody had died,
There were flowers, there were underwater globes,
Mercury seedpearls. It was my mother died.
After a long illness and long ago.

San Pantaleone, heavenly buffoon,
Patron of dotards and of gondolas,
Forgive us the obsessional daydream
Of our redemption at work in black and white,
The silent movie, the old *Commedia*,
Which for the sake of the children in the house
The projectionist has ventured to run backwards.

(The reels must be rewound in any case.)
It is because of jumped, elided frames
That people make their way by jigs and spasms,
Impetuous leapings, violent semaphores,
Side-slipping, drunk discontinuities,
Like the staggered, tossed career of butterflies.
Here, in pure satisfaction of our hunger,
The Keystone Kops sprint from hysteria,
From brisk, slaphappy bludgeonings of crime,
Faultlessly backwards into calm patrol;
And gallons of spilled paint, meekly obedient
As a domestic pet, home in and settle
Securely into casually offered pails,
Leaving the Persian rugs immaculate.
But best of all are the magically dry legs
Emerging from a sudden crater of water
That closes itself up like a healed wound
To plate-glass polish as the diver slides
Upward, attaining with careless arrogance
His unsought footing on the highest board.
Something profoundly soiled, pointlessly hurt
And beyond cure in us yearns for this costless
Ablution, this impossible reprieve,
Unpurchased at a scaffold, free, bequeathed
As rain upon the just and the unjust,
As in the fall of mercy, unconstrained,
Upon the poor, infected place beneath.

II

Elsewhere the spirit is summoned back to life
By bells sifted through floating schools and splices
Of sun-splashed poplar leaves, a reverie
Of light chromatics (Monet and Debussy),
Or the intemperate storms and squalls of traffic,
The coarse, unanswered voice of a fog horn,
Or, best, the shy, experimental aubade

Of the first birds to sense that ashen cold
Grisaille from which the phoenix dawn arises.
Summoned, that is to say, to the world's life
From Piranesian *Carceri* and rat holes
Of its own deep contriving. But here in Venice,
The world's most louche and artificial city
(In which my tale sometime will peter out),
The summons comes from the harsh smashing of glass.
A not unsuitable local industry,
Being the frugal and space-saving work
Of the young men who run the garbage scows.
Wine bottles of a clear sea-water green,
Pale, smoky quarts of *acqua minerale*,
Iodine-tinted liters, the true-blue
Waterman's midnight ink of Bromo-Seltzer,
Light-bulbs of packaged fog, fluorescent tubes
Of well-sealed, antiseptic samples of cloud,
Await what is at once their liquidation
And resurrection in the glory holes
Of the Murano furnaces. Meanwhile
Space must be made for all ephemera,
Our cast-offs, foulings, whatever has gone soft
With age, or age has hardened to a stone,
Our city sweepings. Venice has no curbs
At which to curb a dog, so underfoot
The ocher pastes and puddings of dogshit
Keep us earthbound in half a dozen ways,
Curbing the spirit's tendency to pride.
The palaces decay. Venice is rich
Chiefly in the deposits of her dogs.
A wealth swept up and gathered with its makers.
Canaries, mutts, love-birds and alley cats
Are sacked away like so many Monte Cristos,
There being neither lawns, meadows nor hillsides
To fertilize or to be buried in.
For them the glass is broken in the dark
As a remembrance by the garbage men.

I am their mourner at collection time
With an invented litany of my own.
Wagner died here, Stravinsky's buried here,
They say that Cimarosa's enemies
Poisoned him here. The mind at four a.m.
Is a poor, blotched, vermiculated thing.
I've seen it spilled like sweetbreads, and I've dreamed
Of Byron writing, "Many a fine day
I should have blown my brains out but for the thought
Of the pleasure it would give my mother-in-law."
Thus virtues, it is said, are forced upon us
By our own impudent crimes. I think of him
With his consorts of whores and countesses
Smelling of animal musk, lilac and garlic,
A *ménage* that was in fact a menagerie,
A fox, a wolf, a mastiff, birds and monkeys,
Corbaccios and corvinos, *spintriae*,
The lees of the Venetian underworld,
A plague of iridescent flies. Spilled out.
O lights and livers. Deader than dead weight.
In a casket lined with tufted tea-rose silk.
O that the soul should tie its shoes, the mind
Should wash its hands in a sink, that a small grain
Of immortality should fit itself
With dentures. We slip down by grades and degrees,
Lapses of memory, the vacant eye
And spittled lip, by soiled humiliations
Of mind and body into the last ditch,
Passing, en route to the *Incurabili*,
The backwater way stations of the soul,
Conveyed in the glossy hearse-and-coffin black
And soundless gondola by an overpriced
Apprentice Charon to the *Calle dei Morti*.
One approaches the Venetian underworld
Silently and by water, the gondolier
Creating eddies and whirlpools with each stroke
Like oak roots, silver, smooth and muscular.

One slides to it like a swoon, nearing the regions
Where the vast hosts of the dead mutely inhabit,
Pulseless, indifferent, deeply beyond caring
What shape intrudes itself upon their fathoms.
The oar-blade flings broadcast its beads of light,
Its ordinary gems. One travels past
All of these domiciles of raw sienna,
Burnt umber, colors of the whole world's clays.
One's weakness in itself becomes delicious
Toward the end, a kindly vacancy.
(Raise both your arms above your head, and then
Take three deep breaths, holding the third. Your partner,
Your childhood guide into the other world,
Will approach from behind and wrap you in a bear hug,
Squeezing with all his might. Your head will seethe
With prickled numbness, like an arm or leg
From which the circulation is cut off,
The lungs turn warm with pain, and then you slip
Into a velvet darkness, mutely grateful
To your Anubis-executioner . . .)
Probably I shall die here unremarked
Amid the albergo's seedy furniture,
Aware to the last of the faintly rotten scent
Of swamp and sea, a brief embarrassment
And nuisance to the management and the maid.
That would be bad enough without the fear
Byron confessed to: "If I should reach old age
I'll die 'at the top first,' like Swift." Or Swift's
Lightning-struck tree. There was a visitor,
The little Swiss authority on nightmares,
Young Henry Fuseli, who at thirty-one
Suffered a fever here for several days
From which he recovered with his hair turned white
As a judicial wig, and rendered permanently
Left-handed. And His Majesty, George III,
Desired the better acquaintance of a tree
At Windsor, and heartily shook one of its branches,

Taking it for the King of Prussia. Laugh
Whoso will that has no knowledge of
The violent ward. They subdued that one
With a hypodermic, quickly tranquillized
And trussed him like a fowl. These days I find
A small aperitif at Florian's
Is helpful, although I do not forget.
My views are much like Fuseli's, who described
His method thus: "I first sits myself down.
I then works myself up. Then I throws in
My darks. And then I takes away my lights."
His nightmare was a great success, while mine
Plays on the ceiling of my rented room
Or on the bone concavity of my skull
In the dark hours when I take away my lights.

      Lights. I have chosen Venice for its light,
Its lightness, buoyancy, its calm suspension
In time and water, its strange quietness.
I, an expatriate American,
Living off an annuity, confront
The lagoon's waters in mid-morning sun.
Palladio's church floats at its anchored peace
Across from me, and the great church of Health,
Voted in gratitude by the Venetians
For heavenly deliverance from the plague,
Voluted, levels itself on the canal.
Farther away the bevels coil and join
Like spiralled cordon ropes of silk, the lips
Of the crimped water sped by a light breeze.
Morning has tooled the bay with bright inlays
Of writhing silver, scattered scintillance.
These little crests and ripples promenade,
Hurried and jocular and never bored,
Ils se promènent like families of some means
On Sundays in the *Bois.* Observing this
Easy festivity, hypnotized by

Tiny sun-signals exchanged across the harbor,
I am for the moment cured of everything,
The future held at bay, the past submerged,
Even the fact that this Sea of Hadria,
This consecrated, cool wife of the Doge,
Was ploughed by the merchantmen of all the world,
And all the silicate fragility
They sweat for at the furnaces now seems
An admirable and shatterable triumph.
They take the first crude bulb of thickened glass,
Glowing and taffy-soft on the blow tube,
And sink it in a mold, a metal cup
Spiked on its inner surface like a pineapple.
Half the glass now is regularly dimpled,
And when these dimples are covered with a glaze
Of molten glass they are prisoned air-bubbles,
Breathless, enamelled pearly vacancies.

III

    I am a person of inflexible habits
And comforting rigidities, and though
I am a twentieth-century infidel
From Lawrence, Massachusetts, twice a week
I visit the Cathedral of St. Mark's,
That splendid monument to the labors of
Grave robbers, body snatchers, those lawless two
Entrepreneurial Venetians who
In compliance with the wishes of the Doge
For the greater commercial and religious glory
Of Venice in the year 828
Kidnapped the corpse of the Evangelist
From Alexandria, a sacrilege
The saint seemed to approve. That ancient city
Was drugged and bewildered with an odor of sanctity,
Left powerless and mystified by oils,
Attars and essences of holiness

And roses during the midnight exhumation
And spiriting away of the dead saint
By Buono and his sidekick Rustico—
Goodness in concert with Simplicity
Effecting the major heist of Christendom.

I enter the obscure aquarium dimness,
The movie-palace dark, through which incline
Smoky diagonals and radiant bars
Of sunlight from the high southeastern crescents
Of windowed drums above. Like slow blind fingers
Finding their patient and unvarying way
Across the braille of pavement, edging along
The pavonine and lapidary walls,
Inching through silence as the earth revolves
To huge compulsions, as the turning spheres
Drift in their milky pale galactic light
Through endless quiet, gigantic vacancy,
Unpitying, inhuman, terrible.
In time the eye accommodates itself
To the dull phosphorescence. Gradually
Glories reveal themselves, grave mysteries
Of the faith cast off their shadows, assume their forms
Against a heaven of coined and sequined light,
A splatter of gilt cobblestones, flung grains
Or crumbs of brilliance, the vast open fields
Of the sky turned intimate and friendly. Patines
And laminae, a vermeil shimmering
Of fish-scaled, cataphracted golden plates.
Here are the saints and angels brought together
In studied reveries of happiness.
Enormous wings of seraphim uphold
The crowning domes where the convened apostles
Receive their fiery tongues from the Godhead
Descended to them as a floating dove,
Patriarch and collateral ancestor
Of the pigeons out in the Square. Into those choirs

Of lacquered Thrones, enamelled Archangels
And medalled Principalities rise up
A cool plantation of columns, marble shafts
Bearing their lifted pathways, viaducts
And catwalks through the middle realms of heaven.
Even as God descended into the mass
And thick of us, so is He borne aloft
As promise and precursor to us all,
Ascending in the central dome's vast hive
Of honeyed luminosity. Behind
The altar He appears, two fingers raised
In benediction, in what seems two-thirds
Of the Boy Scout salute, wishing us well.
And we are gathered here below the saints,
Virtues and martyrs, sheltered in their glow,
Soothed by the punk and incense, to rejoice
In the warm light of Gabrieli's horns,
And for a moment of unwonted grace
We are so blessed as to forget ourselves.
Perhaps. There is something selfish in the self,
The cell's craving for perpetuity,
The sperm's ignorant hope, the animal's rule
Of haunch and sinew, testicle and groin,
That refers all things whatever, near and far,
To one's own needs or fantasized desires.
Returning suddenly to the chalk-white sunlight
Of out-of-doors, one spots among the tourists
Those dissolute young with heavy-lidded gazes
Of cool, clear-eyed, stony depravity
That in the course of only a few years
Will fade into the terrifying boredom
In the faces of Carpaccio's prostitutes.
From motives that are anything but kindly
I ignore their indiscreet solicitations
And far more obvious poverty. The mind
Can scarcely cope with the world's sufferings,
Must blinker itself to much or else go mad.

And the bargain that we make for our sanity
Is the knowledge that when at length it comes our turn
To be numbered with the outcasts, the maimed, the poor,
The injured and insulted, they will turn away,
The fortunate and healthy, as I turn now.
(Though touched as much with compassion as with lust,
Knowing the smallest gift would reverse our roles,
Expose me as weak and thus exploitable.
There is more stamina, twenty times more hope
In the least of them than there is left in me.)
I take my loneliness as a vocation,
A policied exile from the human race,
A cultivated, earned misanthropy
After the fashion of the Miller of Dee.

        It wasn't always so. I was an Aid Man,
A Medic with an infantry company,
Who because of my refusal to bear arms
Was constrained to bear the wounded and the dead
From under enemy fire, and to bear witness
To inconceivable pain, usually shot at
Though banded with Red Crosses and unarmed.
There was a corporal I knew in Heavy Weapons,
Someone who carried with him into combat
A book of etiquette by Emily Post.
Most brought with them some token of the past,
Some emblem of attachment or affection
Or coddled childhood—Bibles and baby booties,
Harmonicas, love letters, photographs—
But this was different. I discovered later
That he had been brought up in an orphanage,
So the book was his fiction of kindliness,
A novel in which personages of wealth
Firmly secure domestic tranquillity.
He'd cite me instances. It seems a boy
Will not put "Mr." on his calling cards
Till he leaves school, and may omit the "Mr."

Even while at college. Bread and butter plates
Are never placed on a formal dinner table.
At a simple dinner party one may serve
Claret instead of champagne with the meat.
The satin facings on a butler's lapels
Are narrower than a gentleman's, and he wears
Black waistcoat with white tie, whereas the gentleman's
White waistcoat goes with both black tie and white.
When a lady lunches alone at her own home
In a formally kept house the table is set
For four. As if three Elijahs were expected.
This was to him a sort of *Corpus Juris*,
An ancient piety and governance
Worthy of constant dream and meditation.
He haunts me here, that seeker after law
In a lawless world, in rainsoaked combat boots,
Oil-stained fatigues and heavy bandoleers.
He was killed by enemy machine-gun fire.
His helmet had fallen off. They had sheared away
The top of his cranium like a soft-boiled egg,
And there he crouched, huddled over his weapon,
His brains wet in the chalice of his skull.

IV

    Where to begin? In a heaven of golden serifs
Or smooth and rounded loaves of risen gold,
Formed into formal Caslon capitals
And graced with a pretzelled, sinuous ampersand
Against a sanded ground of fire-truck red,
Proclaiming to the world at large, "The Great
Atlantic & Pacific Tea Co."?
The period alone appeared to me
An eighteen-karat doorknob beyond price.
This was my uncle's store where I was raised.
A shy asthmatic child, I was permitted
To improvise with used potato sacks

Of burlap a divan behind the counter
Where I could lie and read or dream my dreams.
These were infused with the smell of fruit and coffee,
Strong odors of American abundance.
Under the pressed-tin ceiling's coffering
I'd listen to the hissing radiator,
Hung with its can, like a tapped maple tree,
To catch its wrathful spittings, and meditate
On the arcane meaning of the mystic word
(Fixed in white letters backwards on the window)
That referred inscrutably to nothing else
Except itself. An uncracked code: SALADA.
By childhood's rules of inference it concerned
Saladin and the camphors of the East,
And through him, by some cognate lineage
Of sound and mystic pedigree, Aladdin,
A hushed and shadowy world of minarets,
Goldsmiths, persimmons and the ninety-nine
Unutterable Arabian names of God.
I had an eye for cyphers and riddling things.
Of all my schoolmates I was the only one
Who knew that on the bottle of Worcestershire
The conjured names of Lea and Perrins figure
Forty-eight times, weaving around the border
As well as the obvious places front and back.
I became in time a local spelling champion,
Encouraged and praised at home, where emphasis
Was placed on what was then called *elocution*
And upon "building" a vocabulary,
A project that seemed allied to architecture,
The unbuttressed balancing of wooden blocks
Into a Tower of Babel. Still, there were prizes
For papers in my English class: Carlyle
On The Dignity of Labor; John Stuart Mill
On Happiness. But the origin of things
Lies elsewhere. Back in some genetic swamp.

My uncle had worked hard to get his store.
Soon as he could he brought his younger brothers
From the Old Country. My father brought his bride
Of two months to the second-story room
Above the storage. Everybody shared
Labors and profits; they stayed open late
Seven days a week (but closed on Christmas Day)
And did all right. But cutting up the pie
Of measured earnings among five adults
(Four brothers and my mother—I didn't count,
Being one year old at the time) seemed to my father
A burden upon everyone. He announced
That he was going west to make his fortune
And would send soon as he could for mother and me.
Everyone thought him brave and enterprising.
There was a little party, with songs and tears
And special wine, purchased for the occasion.
He left. We never heard from him again.

When I was six years old it rained and rained
And never seemed to stop. I had an oilskin,
A bright sou'wester, stiff and sunflower yellow,
And fireman boots. Rain stippled the windows
Of the school bus that brought us home at dusk
That was no longer dusk but massing dark
As that small world of kids drove into winter,
And always in that dark our grocery store
Looked like a theater or a puppet show,
Lit, warm, and peopled with the family cast,
Full of prop vegetables, a brighter sight
Than anyone else's home. Therefore I knew
Something was clearly up when the bus door
Hinged open and all the lights were on upstairs
But only the bulb at the cash register lit
The store itself, half dark, and on the steps,
Still in his apron, standing in the rain,
My uncle. He was soaked through. He told me

He was taking me to a movie and then to supper
At a restaurant, though the next day was school
And I had homework. It was clear to me
That such a treat exacted on my part
The condition that I shouldn't question it.
We went to see a bedroom comedy,
Let Us Be Gay, scarcely for six-year-olds,
Throughout the length of which my uncle wept.
And then we went to a Chinese restaurant
And sat next to the window where I could see,
Beyond the Chinese equivalent of SALADA
Encoded on the glass, the oil-slicked streets,
The gutters with their little Allagashes
Bent on some urgent mission to the sea.
Next day they told me that my mother was dead.
I didn't go to school. I watched the rain
From the bedroom window or from my burlap nest
Behind the counter. My whole life was changed
Without my having done a single thing.
Perhaps because of those days of constant rain
I am always touched by it now, touched and assuaged.
Perhaps that early vigilance at windows
Explains why I have now come to regard
Life as a spectator sport. But I find peace
In the arcaded dark of the piazza
When a thunderstorm comes up. I watch the sky
Cloud into tarnished zinc, to Quaker grey
Drabness, its shrouded vaults, fog-bound crevasses
Blinking with huddled lightning, and await
The vast *son et lumière.* The city's lamps
Faintly ignite in the gathered winter gloom.
The rumbled thunder starts—an avalanche
Rolling down polished corridors of sound,
Rickety tumbrels blundering across
A stone and empty cellarage. And then,
Like a whisper of dry leaves, the rain begins.
It stains the paving stones, forms a light mist

Of brilliant crystals dulled with tones of lead
Three inches off the ground. Blown shawls of rain
Quiver and luff, veil the cathedral front
In flailing laces while the street lamps hold
Fixed globes of sparkled haze high in the air
And the black pavement runs with wrinkled gold
In pools and wet dispersions, fiery spills
Of liquid copper, of squirming, molten brass.
To give one's whole attention to such a sight
Is a sort of blessedness. No room is left
For antecedence, inference, nuance.
One escapes from all the anguish of this world
Into the refuge of the present tense.
The past is mercifully dissolved, and in
Easy obedience to the gospel's word,
One takes no thought whatever of tomorrow,
The soul being drenched in fine particulars.

      V

    Seeing is misbelieving, as may be seen
By the angled stems, like fractured tibias,
Misplaced by water's anamorphosis.
Think of the blonde with the exposed midriff
Who grins as the cross-cut saw slides through her navel,
Or, better, the wobbled clarity of streams,
Their gravelled bottoms strewn with casual plunder
Of earthen golds, shark greys, palomino browns
Giddily swimming in and out of focus,
Where, in a passing moment of accession,
One thinks one sees in all that spangled bath,
That tarsial, cosmatesque bespattering,
The anchored floating of a giant trout.
All lenses—the corneal tunic of the eye,
Fine scopes and glazier's filaments—mislead us
With insubstantial visions, like objects viewed
Through crizzled and quarrelled panes of Bull's Eye Glass.

It turned out in the end that John Stuart Mill
Knew even less about happiness than I do,
Who know at last, alas, that it is composed
Of clouded, cataracted, darkened sight,
Merciful blindnesses and ignorance.
Only when paradisal bliss had ended
Was enlightenment vouchsafed to Adam and Eve,
"And the eyes of them both were opened, and they knew . . ."
I, for example, though I had lost my parents,
Thought I was happy almost throughout my youth.
Innocent, like Othello in his First Act.
"I saw 't not, thought it not, it harmed not me."
The story I have to tell is only my story
By courtesy of painful inference.
So far as I can tell it, it is true,
Though it has comprised the body of such dreams,
Such broken remnant furnishings of the mind
That my unwilling suspension of disbelief
No longer can distinguish between fact
As something outward, independent, given,
And the enfleshment of disembodied thought,
Some melanotic malevolence of my own.
I know this much for sure: When I was eighteen
My father returned home. In a boxcar, dead.
I learned, or else I dreamed, that heading west
He got no farther than Toledo, Ohio,
Where late one night in a vacant parking lot
He was robbed, hit on the head with a quart bottle,
Left bleeding and unconscious and soaked with rum
By a couple of thugs who had robbed a liquor store
And found in my father, besides his modest savings,
A convenient means of diverting the police.
He came to in the hospital, walletless,
Paperless, without identity.
He had no more than a dozen words of English
Which, in hysterical anxiety
Or perhaps from the concussion, evaded him.

The doctors seemed to be equally alarmed
By possible effects of the blow to his head
And by his wild excitability
In a tongue nobody there could understand.
He was therefore transferred for observation
To the State Mental Hospital where he stayed
Almost a year before, by merest chance,
A visitor of Lithuanian background
Heard and identified his Lettish speech,
And it could be determined that he was
In full possession of his faculties,
If of little else, and where he had come from
And all the rest of it. The Toledo police
Then wrote my uncle a letter. Without unduly
Stressing their own casualness in the matter,
They told my uncle where his brother was,
How he had come to be there, and that because
He had no funds or visible means of support
He would be held pending a money order
That should cover at least his transportation home.
They wrote three times. They didn't get an answer.

The immigrants to Lawrence, Massachusetts,
Were moved as by the vision of Isaiah
To come to the New World, to become new
And enter into a peaceful Commonwealth.
This meant hard work, a scrupulous adoption
Of local ways, endeavoring to please
Clients and neighbors, to become at length,
Despite the ineradicable stigma
Of a thick accent, one like all the rest,
Homogenized and inconspicuous.
So much had the prophetic vision come to.
It would not do at all to have it known
That any member of the family
Had been in police custody, or, worse,
In an asylum. All the kind good will

And friendly custom of the neighborhood
Would be withdrawn at the mere breath of scandal.
Prudence is one of the New England virtues
My uncle was at special pains to learn.
And it paid off, as protestant virtue does,
In cold coin of the realm. Soon he could buy
His own store and take his customers with him
From the A. & P. By the time I was in high school
He and his brothers owned a modest chain
Of little grocery stores and butcher shops.
And he took on as well the unpaid task
Of raising me, making himself my parent,
Forbearing and encouraging and kind.
Or so it seemed. Often in my nightmares
Since then I appear craven and repulsive,
Always soliciting his good opinion
As he had sought that of the neighborhood.
The dead keep their own counsel, let nothing slip
About incarceration, so it was judged
Fitting to have the funeral back home.
Home now had changed. We lived, uncle and I,
In a whole house of our own with a German cook.
The body was laid out in the living room
In a casket lined with tufted tea-rose silk,
Upholstered like a Victorian love-seat.
He had never been so comfortable. He looked
Almost my age, more my age than my uncle's,
Since half his forty years had not been lived,
Had merely passed, like birthdays or the weather.
He was, strangely enough, a total stranger
Who bore a clear family resemblance.
And there was torture in my uncle's face
Such as I did not even see at war.
The flowers were suffocating. It was like drowning.
The day after the burial I enlisted,
And two and a half years later was mustered out
As a Section Eight, mentally unsound.

VI

What is our happiest, most cherished dream
Of paradise? Not harps and fugues and feathers
But rather arrested action, an escape
From time, from history, from evolution
Into the blessèd stasis of a painting:
Those tributes, homages, apotheoses
Figured upon the ceilings of the rich
Wherein some rather boorish-looking count,
With game leg and bad breath, roundly despised
By all of his contemporaries, rises
Into the company of the heavenly host
(A pimpled donor among flawless saints)
Viewed by us proletarians on the floor
From under his thick ham and dangled calf
As he is borne beyond our dark resentment
On puffy quilts and comforters of cloud.
Suspended always at that middle height
In numinous diffusions of soft light,
In mild soft-focus, in the "tinted steam"
Of Turner's visions of reality,
He is established at a pitch of triumph,
That shall not fail him, by the painter's skill.
Yet in its way even the passage of time
Seems to inch toward a vast and final form,
To mimic the grand metastasis of art,
As if all were ordained. As the writ saith:
The fathers (and their brothers) shall eat grapes
And the teeth of the children shall be set on edge.
Ho fatto un fiasco, which is to say,
I've made a sort of bottle of my life,
A frangible and a transparent failure.
My efforts at their best are negative:
A poor attempt not to hurt anyone,
A goal which, in the very nature of things,
Is ludicrous because impossible.
Viscid, contaminate, dynastic wastes
Flood through the dark canals, the underpasses,

Ducts and arterial sluices of my body
As through those gutters of which Swift once wrote:
"Sweepings from Butcher Stalls, Dung, Guts, and Blood,
Drown'd Puppies, stinking Sprats, all drench'd in Mud,
Dead Cats and Turnip-Tops come tumbling down the Flood."
At least I pass them on to nobody,
Not having married, or authored any children,
Leading a monkish life of modest means
On a trust fund established by my uncle
In a will of which I am the single heir.
I am not young any more, and not very well,
Subject to nightmares and to certain fevers
The doctors cannot cure. There's a Madonna
Set in an alley shrine near where I live
Whose niche is filled with little votive gifts,
Like cookie molds, of pressed tin eyes and legs
And organs she has mercifully cured.
She is not pretty, she is not high art,
But in my infidel way I'm fond of her—
Saint Mary Paregoric, Comforter.
Were she to cure me, what could I offer her?
The gross, intestinal wormings of the brain?

        A virus's life-span is twenty minutes.
Think of its evolutionary zeal,
Like the hyper-active balance-wheel of a watch,
Busy with swift mutations, trundling through
Its own Silurian epochs in a week;
By fierce ambition and Darwinian wit
Acquiring its immunities against
Our warfares and our plagues of medication.
Blessed be the unseen micro-organisms,
For without doubt they shall inherit the earth.
Their generations shall be as the sands of the sea.
I am the dying host by which they live;
In me they dwell and thrive and have their being.
I am the tapered end of a long line,

The thin and febrile phylum of my family:
Of all my father's brothers the one child.
I wander these by-paths and little squares,
A singular Tyrannosaurus Rex,
Sauntering toward extinction, an obsolete
Left-over from a weak *ancien régime*
About to be edged out by upstart germs.
I shall pay out the forfeit with my life
In my own lingering way. Just as my uncle,
Who, my blood tells me on its nightly rounds,
May perhaps be "a little more than kin,"
Has paid the price for his unlawful grief
And bloodless butchery by creating me
His guilty legatee, the beneficiary
Of his money and his crimes.
                              In these late days
I find myself frequently at the window,
Its glass a cooling comfort to my temple.
And I lift up mine eyes, not to the hills
Of which there are not any, but to the clouds.
Here is a sky determined to maintain
The reputation of Tiepolo,
A moving vision of a shapely mist,
Full of the splendor of the insubstantial.
Against a diorama of palest blue
Cloud-curds, cloud-stacks, cloud-bushes sun themselves.
Giant confections, impossible meringues,
Soft coral reefs and powdery tumuli
Pass in august processions and calm herds.
Great stadiums, grandstands and amphitheaters,
The tufted, opulent litters of the gods
They seem; or laundered bunting, well-dressed wigs,
Harvests of milk-white, Chinese peonies
That visibly rebuke our stinginess.
For all their ghostly presences, they take on
A colorful nobility at evening.
Off to the east the sky begins to turn

Lilac so pale it seems a mood of grey,
Gradually, like the death of virtuous men.
Streaks of electrum richly underline
The slow, flat-bottomed hulls, those floated lobes
Between which quills and spokes of light fan out
Into carnelian reds and nectarines,
Nearing a citron brilliance at the center,
The searing furnace of the glory hole
That fires and fuses clouds of muscatel
With pencillings of gold. I look and look,
As though I could be saved simply by looking—
I, who have never earned my way, who am
No better than a viral parasite,
Or the lees of the Venetian underworld,
Foolish and muddled in my later years,
Who was never even at one time a wise child.

from THE TRANSPARENT MAN

CURRICULUM VITAE

As though it were reluctant to be day,
    Morning deploys a scale
    Of rarities in grey,
And winter settles down in its chain-mail,

Victorious over legions of gold and red.
    The smoky souls of stones,
    Blunt pencillings of lead,
Pare down the world to glintless monotones

Of graveyard weather, vapors of a fen
    We reckon through our pores.
    Save for the garbage men,
Our children are the first ones out of doors.

Book-bagged and padded out, at mouth and nose
    They manufacture ghosts,
    George Washington's and Poe's,
Banquo's, the Union and Confederate hosts',

And are themselves the ghosts, file-cabinet grey,
    Of some departed us,
    Signing our lives away
On ferned and parslied windows of a bus.

CHORUS FROM *OEDIPUS AT COLONOS*

What is unwisdom but the lusting after
Longevity: to be old and full of days!
For the vast and unremitting tide of years
Casts up to view more sorrowful things than joyful;
And as for pleasures, once beyond our prime,
They all drift out of reach, they are washed away.
And the same gaunt bailiff calls upon us all,
Summoning into Darkness, to those wards
Where is no music, dance, or marriage hymn
That soothes or gladdens. To the tenements of Death.

Not to be born is, past all yearning, best.
And second best is, having seen the light,
To return at once to deep oblivion.
When youth has gone, and the baseless dreams of youth,
What misery does not then jostle man's elbow,
Join him as a companion, share his bread?
Betrayal, envy, calumny and bloodshed
Move in on him, and finally Old Age—
Infirm, despised Old Age—joins in his ruin,
The crowning taunt of his indignities.

So is it with that man, not just with me.
He seems like a frail jetty facing North
Whose pilings the waves batter from all quarters;
From where the sun comes up, from where it sets,
From freezing boreal regions, from below,
A whole winter of miseries now assails him,
Thrashes his sides and breaks over his head.

TERMS

for Derek Walcott

Holidays, books and lives draw to their close,
The curtain rings down on some theater piece,
The brass, string, and percussion sections close
In on their tonic and concordant close
When all loose ends infallibly are tied
Into baroque or plain completion. Close
Your eyes, and a childhood landscape wades in close
With delicate birch to supplant the frank disgrace
Of our littoral, littered world, as painters grace
A woman's grief, a beggar's bowl, with close
Clear scrutiny until a world has grown
Out of Rembrandt's pain and a narrow ghetto's groan.

Open your eyes. A body of water has grown
Obsidian, slick and ballroom smooth. Look close,
And, through a wind's light pucker, mark full-grown
Migrations of clouds, to which small fish have grown
Accustomed, which they inhabit, all of a piece
With their rock-bottom skies. And now the grown
Wind-wrinkles, the mackerel heavens, with their ingrown
Pisces and constellated summertide,
Calm for an instant, arresting the whole tide
Of time, like ants in amber, momently grown
Changeless and still as painting, fluttering grace
Notes that are held in mind by an act of grace.

The young are full of an astonishing grace,
Soft-eyed, trustful and lithe till they have grown
Aware of being admired for their grace,
Whereupon they go through some fall from grace,
An aging that reminds us of our close.
The skater's tilt, the contemplator's grace
Are both a selflessness, evincing grace
In agile tension as well as mastered peace,
In a poise of speed or stillness. But our last peace,

Stone-capped, dark-rooted, engraved and void of grace,
Beds down in rain and rubble, and eventide
Sees us unsinewed, our last lank strands untied.

What do those distant thunderheads betide?
Nothing to do with us. Not our disgrace
That the raped corpse of a fourteen-year-old, tied
With friction tape, is found in a ditch, and a tide
Of violent crime breaks out. Yet the world grown
Wrathful, corrupt, once loosed a true floodtide
That inched inside the wards where the frail are tied
To their beds, invaded attics, climbed to disclose
Sharks in the nurseries, eels on the floors, to close
Over lives and cries and herds, and on that tide,
Which splintered barn, cottage and city piece-
Meal, one sole family rode the world to peace.

Think of the glittering morning when God's peace
Flooded the heavens as it withdrew the tide:
Sweet grasses, endless fields of such rich peace
That for long after, when men dreamed of peace,
It seemed a place where beast and human grace
A pastoral landscape, a Virgilian peace,
Or scene such as Mantegna's masterpiece
Of kneeling shepherds. But that dream has grown
Threadbare, improbable, and our paupers groan
While "stockpiled warheads guarantee our peace,"
And troops, red-handed, muscle in for the close.
Ours is a wound that bleeds and will not close.

Long since we had been cautioned: "Until he close
His eyes forever, mildly and in peace,
Call no man happy." The stain of our disgrace
Grows ominously, a malign, ingrown
Melanoma, softly spreading its dark tide.

DEVOTIONS OF A PAINTER

Cool sinuosities, waved banners of light,
Unfurl, remesh, and round upon themselves
In a continuing turmoil of benign
Cross-purposes, effortlessly as fish,
On the dark underside of the foot-bridge,
Cast upward against pewter-weathered planks.
Weeds flatten with the current. Dragonflies
Poise like blue needles, steady in mid-air,
For some decisive, swift inoculation.
The world repeats itself in ragged swatches
Among the lily-pads, but understated,
When observed from this selected vantage point,
A human height above the water-level,
As the shore shelves heavily over its reflection,
Its timid, leaf-strewn comment on itself.
It's midday in midsummer. Pitiless heat.
Not so much air in motion as to flutter
The frail, bright onion tissue of a poppy.
I am an elderly man in a straw hat
Who has set himself the task of praising God
For all this welter by setting out my paints
And getting as much truth as can be managed
Onto a small flat canvas. Constable
Claimed he had never seen anything ugly,
And would have known each crushed jewel in the pigments
Of these oily golds and greens, enamelled browns
That recall the glittering eyes and backs of frogs.
The sun dispenses its immense loose change,
Squandered on blossoms, ripples, mud, wet stones.
I am enamored of the pale chalk dust
Of the moth's wing, and the dark moldering gold
Of rust, the corrupted treasures of this world.
Against the Gospel let my brush declare:
"These are the anaglyphs and gleams of love."

DESTINATIONS

The harvest is past, the summer is ended,
and we are not saved.

       —JEREMIAH

The children having grown up and moved away,
One day she announced in brisk and scathing terms
That since for lo, as she said, these many years
She had thanklessly worked her fingers to the bone,
Always put him and the children first and foremost
(A point he thought perhaps disputable),
She had had it up to here, and would be leaving
The following day, would send him an address
To which her belongings could be forwarded
And to which the monthly payments could be sent.
He could see her point. It was only tit for tat.
After all the years when the monthly pains were hers
They now were to be his. True to her word,
Which she commanded him to mark, she packed
And left, and took up shifting residence,
First with a barber, then with a state trooper:
From the scissors of severance to the leather holster
Of the well-slung groin—the six-pack, six-gun weapon
Of death and generation. He could see the point.
In these years of inflation ways and means
Had become meaner and more chancy ways
Of getting along. Economy itself
Urged perfect strangers to bed down together
Simply to make ends meet, and so ends met.
Rather to his surprise, his first reaction
Was a keen sense of relief and liberation.
It seemed that, thinking of her, he could recall
Only a catalogue of pettiness,
Selfishness, spite, a niggling litany
Of minor acrimony, punctuated
By outbursts of hysteria and violence.
Now there was peace, the balm of Gilead,
At least at first. Slowly it dawned upon him
That she had no incentive to remarry,

Since, by remaining single and shacking up,
She would enjoy two sources of income.
In the house of her deferred and mortgaged dreams
Two lived as cheaply as one, if both had funds.
He thought about this off and on for years
As he went on subsidizing her betrayal
In meek obedience to the court decree,
And watered the flowers by his chain-link fence
Beside the railroad tracks. In his back yard
He kept petunias in a wooden tub
Inside the whitewashed tire of a tractor trailer,
And his kitchen steps of loose, unpainted boards
Afforded him an unimpeded view
Of the webbed laundry lines of all his neighbors,
Rusted petroleum tins, the buckled wheels
Of abandoned baby-carriages, and the black-
Sooted I-beams and girders of a bridge
Between two walls of rusticated stonework
Through which the six-fifteen conveyed the lucky
And favored to superior destinies.
Where did they go, these fortunates? He'd seen
Blonde, leggy girls pouting invitingly
In low-cut blouses on TV commercials,
And thought about encountering such a one
In a drugstore or supermarket. She
Would smile (according to his dream scenario)
And come straight home with him as if by instinct.
But in the end, he knew, this would be foreplay
To the main event when she'd take him to the cleaners.

MEDITATION

for William Alfred

Quattrocento put in paint
On backgrounds for a God or Saint
Gardens where a soul's at ease;
Where everything that meets the eye,
Flowers and grass and cloudless sky,
Resemble forms that are or seem
When sleepers wake and yet still dream,
And when it's vanished still declare,
With only bed and bedstead there,
That heavens had opened.

I

The orchestra tunes up, each instrument
In lunatic monologue putting on its airs,
Oblivious, haughty, full of self-regard.
The flute fingers its priceless strand of pearls,
Nasal disdain is eructed by the horn,
The strings let drop thin overtones of malice,
Inchoate, like the dense garbling of voices
At a cocktail party, which the ear sorts out
By alert exclusions, keen selectivities.
A five-way conversation, at its start
Smooth and intelligible as a Brahms quintet,
Disintegrates after one's third martini
To dull orchestral nonsense, the jumbled fragments
Of domestic friction in a foreign tongue,
Accompanied by a private sense of panic:
This surely must be how old age arrives,
Quite unannounced, when suddenly one fine day
Some trusted faculty has gone forever.

II

After the closing of cathedral doors,
After the last soft footfall fades away,
There still remain artesian, grottoed sounds
Below the threshold of the audible,
The infinite, unspent reverberations
Of the prayers, coughs, whispers and *amens* of the day,
Afloat upon the marble surfaces.
They continue forever. Nothing is ever lost.
So the sounds of children, enriched, magnified,
Cross-fertilized by the contours of a tunnel,
Promote their little statures for a moment
Of resonance to authority and notice,
A fleeting, bold celebrity that rounds
In perfect circles to attentive shores,
Returning now in still enlarging arcs
To which there is no end. Whirled without end.

III

This perfect company is here engaged
In what is called a sacred conversation.
A seat has been provided for the lady
With her undiapered child in a bright loggia
Floored with *antico verde* and alabaster
Which are cool and pleasing to the feet of saints
Who stand at either side. It is eight o'clock
On a sunny April morning, and there is much here
Worthy of observation. First of all,
No one in all the group seems to be speaking.
The Baptist, in a rude garment of hides,

Vaguely unkempt, is looking straight at the viewer
With serious interest, patient and unblinking.
Across from him, relaxed but powerful,
Stands St. Sebastian, who is neither a ruse
To get a young male nude with classic torso
Into an obviously religious painting,
Nor one who suffers his target martyrdom
Languidly or with a masochist's satisfaction.
He experiences a kind of acupuncture
That in its blessedness has set him free
To attend to everything except himself.
Jerome and Francis, the one in his red hat,
The other tonsured, both of them utterly silent,
Cast their eyes downward as in deep reflection.
Perched on a marble dais below the lady
A small seraphic consort of viols and lutes
Prepares to play or actually is playing.
They exhibit furrowed, childlike concentration.
A landscape of extraordinary beauty
Leads out behind the personages to where
A shepherd tends his flock. Far off a ship
Sets sail for the world of commerce. Travellers
Kneel at a wayside shrine near a stone wall.
Game-birds or song-birds strut or take the air
In gliding vectors among cypress spires
By contoured vineyards or groves of olive trees.
A belfry crowns a little knoll behind which
The world recedes into a cobalt blue
Horizon of remote, fine mountain peaks.

    The company, though they have turned their backs
To all of this, are aware of everything.
Beneath their words, but audible, the silver
Liquidities of stream and song-bird fall
In cleansing passages, and the water-wheel
Turns out its measured, periodic creak.
They hear the coughs, the raised voices of children

Joyful in the dark tunnel, everything.
Observe with care their tranquil pensiveness.
They hear all the petitions, all the cries
Reverberating over marble floors,
Floating above still water in dark wells.
All the world's woes, all the world's woven woes,
The warp of ages, they hear and understand,
To which is added a final bitterness:
That their own torments, deaths, renunciations,
Made in the name of love, have served as warrant,
Serve to this very morning as fresh warrant
For the infliction of new atrocities.
All this they know. Nothing is ever lost.
It is the condition of their blessedness
To hear and recall the recurrent cries of pain
And parse them into a discourse that consorts
In strange agreement with the viols and lutes,
Which, with the water and the meadow bells,
And every gathered voice, every *amen*,
Join to compose the sacred conversation.

SEE NAPLES AND DIE

It is better to say, "I'm suffering," than to say,
"This landscape is ugly."

—SIMONE WEIL

I

I can at last consider those events
Almost without emotion, a circumstance
That for many years I'd scarcely have believed.
We forget much, of course, and, along with facts,
Our strong emotions, of pleasure and of pain,
Fade into stark insensibility.
For which, perhaps, it need be said, thank God.
So I can read from my journal of that time
As if it were written by a total stranger.
Here is a sunny day in April, the air
Cool as spring water to breathe, but the sun warm.
We are seated under a trellised roof of vines,
Light-laced and freaked with grape-leaf silhouettes
That romp and buck across the tablecloth,
Flicker and slide on the white porcelain.
The air is scented with fresh rosemary,
Boxwood and lemon and a light perfume
From fields of wild-flowers far beyond our sight.
The cheap knives blind us. In the poet's words,
It is almost time for lunch. And the *padrone*
Invites us into blackness the more pronounced
For the brilliance of outdoors. Slowly our eyes
Make out his pyramids of delicacies—
The Celtic coils and curves of primrose shrimp,
A speckled gleam of opalescent squid,
The mussel's pearl-blue niches, as unearthly
As Brazilian butterflies, and the grey turbot,
Like a Picasso lady with both eyes
On one side of her face. We are invited
To choose our fare from this august display
Which serves as menu, and we return once more
To the sunshine, to the fritillary light
And shadow of our table where carafes

Of citrine wine glow with unstable gems,
Prison the sun like genii in their holds,
Enshrine their luminous spirits.
                                        There, before us,
The greatest amphitheater in the world:
Naples and its Bay. We have begun
Our holiday, Martha and I, in rustic splendor.
I look at her with love (was it with love?)
As a breeze takes casual liberties with her hair,
And set it down that evening in the hotel
(Where I make my journal entries after dinner)
That everything we saw this afternoon
After our splendid lunch with its noble view—
The jets of water, Diana in porphyry,
Callipygian, broad-bottomed Venus,
Whole groves of lemons, the packed grenadine pearls
Of pomegranate seeds, olive trees, urns,
All fired and flood-lit by this southern sun—
Bespoke an unassailable happiness.
And so it was. Or so I thought it was.
I believe that on that height I was truly happy,
Though I know less and less as time goes on
About what happiness is, unless it's what
Folk-wisdom celebrates as ignorance.
Dante says that the worst of all torments
Is to remember happiness once it's passed.
I am too numb to know whether he's right.

        II

Over the froth-white cowls of our morning coffee
I read to Martha from a battered guidebook
Which quotes a seventeenth-century diarist,
Candid and down-to-earth, on Naples' whores.
The city, he declared, proudly maintained
A corps of thirty thousand registered sinners,
Taxed and inspected, issued licenses

For the custom of their bodies. One may assume
Their number, and the revenues of the state,
Must have compounded since those early days.
There were accounts, as well, of female beggars
With doped and rented children, and a rich trade
In pathos by assorted mendicants.
Baedeker, who is knowing in these matters,
Warns travellers against misguided kindness:
The importunate should be rebuffed with *niente,*
He firmly advises, and goes on to say
That poverty is a feature of the landscape.
Perhaps this strong fiduciary theme
Prompted attention to our own resources.
A six- or seven-year-old good-looking urchin
Had posted himself each day across the street
From our hotel, and from this vantage point
He offered tourists good black-market rates
Of currency exchange. I fell for this
For what, I suppose, are all the usual reasons.
There was first of all the charming oddity
Of a child-financier plying his trade
With such bright confidence. There was my pride,
The standard, anxious pride of every tourist,
Of wishing to exhibit worldly cunning
And not be subject to official rates.
And there was finally the curious lure
Of doing something questionably legal,
Which I could have no chance to do at home.
So I let the boy guide me through dark back alleys
To a small, grim, unprepossessing square,
Festooned with drying sheets and undergarments
Strung like blank banners high above our heads,
The ensigns of our nameless, furtive business.
He motioned me to wait, and disappeared.
There were two men across the square from me,
Conspicuous, vaguely thuggish, badly dressed,
In lively discourse, paying me no notice,

But filling me with a mild apprehension.
I could hear the whines of children, the louder wails
Of ambulances on their urgent missions
Somewhere far off, claiming their right of way.
The area smelled of garlic, soap, and urine.
And then young Ercole made his appearance.
He introduced himself. He was short, dark,
Athletic, with an air of insolence.
He was neatly dressed with very expensive shoes
In which he evidently took some pride,
A complex wrist-watch boasting several dials,
And delicate hands decked with a dazzle of rings.
Pride, as it seems, was governing us both.
I felt distinctly uncertain of myself
But saw no way before me to withdraw.
I noticed that as our talk got underway
The men across the square had ceased conversing
And were giving us their full consideration,
Which, given the cautious nature of our dealings,
Was far from reassuring. But Ercole,
Who seemed aware that we were being watched,
Was undismayed, and so I went along.
We came to terms. I had my travellers' checks,
And he had bills of large denominations
Rolled into wads, stuffed in his jacket pockets.
He mockingly let me examine one.
It seemed genuine enough. I agreed to exchange
Two hundred dollars' worth of travellers' checks.
He counted out the bills before my eyes,
Folded them neatly into a thick packet,
And I in turn carefully signed my checks,
And we made our exchange. And then he smiled
A smile of condescension and insolence,
Waved to me with a well-manicured hand
On which he wore a number of gold rings
And disappeared. Throughout this both of us
Knew we had been intensively observed

By the two thugs who stood across the square.
They must have seen the large bulge in my pocket
And I was now certainly too mistrustful
To count the bills once more in sight of them
Or ask of them the way to my hotel.
So I made the return home by trial and error,
And only within the confines of my room
Did I discover that my wad of bills
Was almost wholly folded newspaper.
At first, of course, I was furious; Martha thought me
A gullible fool, which didn't improve my mood.
Two hundred dollars is not a trifling sum,
But after a while I began to realize
That Ercole's fine clothes were the pathetic
Costume and *bella figura* of the poor.
For him, like other Neapolitan sinners,
Staying alive, the sheer act of survival,
Was a game of cunning I was quite unused to
And involved paying off confederates:
The helpless urchin outside our hotel,
The two thuggish observers, whose mere presence
Had kept me from discovering the fraud
Until too late, and may have distracted me
(I pride myself on being a keen observer)
From the skilled legerdemain of those adept,
Tapered, manicured, bejewelled hands.

III

See, what a perfect day. It's perhaps three
In the afternoon, if one may judge by the light.
Windless and tranquil, with enough small clouds
To seem like innocent, grazing flocks of heaven.
The air is bright with a thickness of its own,
Enveloping the cool and perfect land,
Where earthly flocks wander and graze at peace
And men converse at ease beside a road

Leading to towers, to battlements and hills,
As a farmer guides his cattle through a maze
Of the chipped and broken headstones of the dead.
All this, serene and lovely as it is,
Serves as mere background to Bellini's painting
Of *The Transfiguration*. Five dazzled apostles,
Three as if just awakening from sleep,
Surround a Christ whose eyes seem to be fixed
On something just behind and above our heads,
Invisible unless we turned, and then
The mystery would indeed still be behind us.
A rear-view mirror might perhaps reveal
Something we cannot see, outside the picture
But yet implied by all Bellini's art.
Whatever it is seems to be understood
By the two erect apostles, one being Peter,
The other possibly John, both of them holding
Fragments of scroll with Hebrew lettering,
Which they appear just to have been consulting.
Their lowered eyes indicate that, unseeing,
They have seen everything, have understood
The entire course of human history,
The meaning and the burden of the lives
Of Samson, Jonah, and Melchizedek,
Isaiah's and Zechariah's prophecies,
The ordinance of destiny, the flow
And tide of providential purposes.
All hope, all life, all effort has assembled
And taken human shape in the one figure
There in the midst of them this afternoon.
And what event could be more luminous?
His birth had been at night, and at his death
The skies would darken, graves give up their dead.
But here, between, was a day so glorious
As to explain and even justify
All human misery and suffering.
Or so, at least, perhaps, the artist felt,

And so we feel, gazing upon a world
From which all pain has cleanly been expunged
By a pastoral hand, moving in synchronous
Obedience to a clear and pastoral eye.
        By this time, having gazed upon as much
Painting in the *Museo Nazionale*
As could reasonably be taken in
On a single morning, we make our way outside
Only to be confronted by the *pompe*
Funebri of six jet-black harnessed chargers,
Each with black ostrich plumes upon his head,
Drawing a carriage-hearse, also beplumed,
Black but glass-walled, and bearing a black coffin
Piled with disorderly hot-house profusions
Of lilies, gladioli, and carnations.
The sidewalk throngs all cross themselves, and Martha
Seems especially and mysteriously upset
In ways I fail to understand until
Back in our room she breaks out angrily:
"Didn't you see how small the coffin was?"
I am bewildered by this accusation.
Of course I *saw*, but thought it far more prudent
To leave the topic delicately untouched.
I am annoyed at her and at myself,
An irritation I must not let damage
What yet remains of this holiday of ours.

        IV

Two days of rain. Confining. Maddening.
From our French windows and our small *balcon*
We watch the cold, unchanging, snake-skinned bay
Curtained by leaden sheets of rain in which
Capri and Procida are set adrift
Beyond the limits of sight, like the *Wandering Isles*.
We are housebound, quarantined. We read and fret,
Trying our best to be cheerful and good humored,

And it occurs to me that only a nation
Devoted to the cult of the Madonna
With all its doctrinal embellishments
Could produce "extra-virgin olive oil."
Martha is not amused by this; the rain
Has damped her spirits, and she has been reading
Grand-Guignol sections on Tiberius
In Suetonius' gossipy old book.
The weather itself feels like those steel engravings
Of the *Inferno* by Gustave Doré:
A ruthless, colorless, unvarying grey.
So that when sunshine comes we are astonished,
Filled with both gratitude and with amazement
At the brilliant flowers in the public squares.
We elect to spend the morning simply sunning
In the great park of the *Villa Nazionale,*
And find ourselves almost restored to normal
When we become reluctant witnesses
To a straggling parade of freaks and mutants
From a local hospital for the handicapped
On a brief outing to the aquarium.
They are extraordinary: stunted, maimed,
Thalidomide deformities, small, fingerless,
Mild pigmentless albinos, shepherded
Into a squeaky file by earnest nuns
Between the sunlit bushes of azaleas.
They seem like raw material for the painting
Of Bosch's *Temptation of St. Anthony:*
Wild creatures, partly human, but with claws
Or camel humps, or shrivelled, meager heads.
What they will see inside those glassy tanks
(Thick sullen eels, pale sea-anemones)
Will be no odder than what they are themselves.
Martha, who never ventures anywhere
Without me, and has not a word of Italian,
Has disappeared.

              I am deeply alarmed.

It suddenly seemed that she might be the victim
Of some barbaric or unthinkable crime:
That, kidnapped, she was being held for ransom,
Or worse. I hurried back to the hotel,
And found her, deeply shaken, in our room,
Unwilling to talk, unwilling, at first, to listen
To any attempt to soothe or comfort her.
I tried to tell her in what must have been
A way that somehow frightened or offended
That life required us to steel ourselves
To the all-too-sad calamities of others,
The brute, inexplicable inequities,
To form for ourselves a carapace of sorts,
A self-preservative petrific toughness.
At this she raised her arm, shielding her eyes
As if she thought I were about to strike her,
And said *No* several times, not as a statement,
But rather as a groan. And then she gave me
A look the like of which I can't describe.
I left her in possession of the room
And spent the rest of the day pacing the lobby,
Taking my tea alone. She finally joined me
For a dinner at which not a word was uttered
On either side.
                        What struck me during the meal
(As if confirming everything I'd told her)
Was a vivid recollection from that morning:
Not of the warped and crippled, but of the reds,
Among the pale profusions of azaleas,
The brilliant reds of the geraniums.

        V

Somewhere along in here, deeply depressed,
I ceased making journal entries, so what follows
Is pretty much an uncertain reconstruction
Concerning our brief excursion to the baths

Of Nero and the surrounding countryside.
It was intended as a light diversion
Into the realms of luxury and ease,
A little apolaustic interval.
Were we wrong, I wonder, to expect so much?
I looked at the map, and saw the *Mare Morto*,
And innocently thought of the Holy Land.
We entrusted ourselves meekly to the hands
Of a guide (found for us by our concierge),
An older man of dignified appearance
Who spoke fair English and was named Raimondo.
His smile was reassuring; we were both
Impressed and pleased by his enthusiasm.
Baiae was once a fashionable resort.
Caesar and Nero and Caligula
Had built their summer villas on this coast.
But Nero's baths were desultory ruins,
Tangled in chicory and acanthus growth,
Littered by tourists, and excrement of dogs.
The hills around are honey-combed with caves,
And Raimondo told us with naive excitement
Of the Sibyl's Cave, the old worldly-wise Sibyl
Who cunningly foxed and outwitted Tarquin,
Obliging him to buy her three last books
For the full price of nine by coolly burning
A set of volumes each time he refused.
But first Raimondo had another cave
Picked for our delectation: damp and foul-smelling,
It was, of course, the well-known *Grotta del Cane*,
Known in the ancient texts as *Charon's Cave*.
The brimstone odors here rise from a depth
No one can measure, keeping the very earth
Throughout this region perpetually warm—
So much that when Raimondo cut some turf
With a penknife and handed me a clod
I could feel heat from subterranean fires.
It's to these bottomless thermal wells of warmth

That all this region owes its opulence,
Its endless summer *wo die Zitronen blühn*.
A man and a mongrel now enter the cave,
Answering Raimondo's summons. We are to view
The ghastly and traditional death-scene.
But only after the no less traditional
And ceremonious haggling about fees,
A routine out of *commedia dell'arte*.
And then, by the scruff of the neck, the master forces
His dog's head close to a rank and steaming fissure
Where fumes rise from the earth, the stink of Dis,
That place of perfect hospitality
"Whose ancient door stands open night and day."
The dog's eyes widen in unseeing terror;
It yelps feebly, goes into wild convulsions,
And then falls limp with every semblance of
Death. Being then removed and laid
Near the cave's mouth, in about thirty seconds
It starts to twitch and drool, then shakes itself,
And presently staggers to its four feet.
With a broad wink and conspiratorial smile,
Raimondo says that by modest computation
That dog dies three hundred times a year,
And has been earning its own livelihood
As well as its owner's for about three years.
This puts it well ahead of Lazarus,
Orpheus, and the others who have made
Sensational returns. As the Sibyl said
Solemnly to Aeneas, "The way down
Is easy from Avernus—but getting back
Requires a certain amount of toil and trouble."
Avernus, as it happens, the stinking lake
No bird can fly across, all birds avoid,
Lies within easy access, as does the Cave
Of Cumaean Sibyl, both of which Raimondo
Encourages us to visit, but we insist
That we have had enough of caves and smells

To last us for a while, so he proposes
A little tour of the Elysian Fields,
The region of the blurred and blissful dead.
Virgil had made it seem a lovely place,
A heroes' health-club, a gymnasium
Of track-stars, wrestlers, athletes, all engaged
In friendly contest, suntanned rivalry.
Here, too, convened all those distinguished ghosts
Who had bettered life by finding out new truths,
Inventing melodies or making verses,
At home in a faultless landscape of green meadows
Watered by streams of dazzling clarity.
What we saw was something different. There was, of course,
No fabulous descent to a nether world.
Instead Raimondo took us to a place
Where, we assumed, he meant to let us pause
Before some planned approach to the sublime.
But he said to us, quite lamely, "This is it.
This is the place called the Elysian Fields."
(I checked his claim that evening in the guidebook,
And the map proved that he had told the truth.)
It was a vacant wilderness of weeds,
Thistles and mulberries, with here and there
Poplars, quite shadeless; thick, ramshackle patches
Of thorny amaranth, tousled by vines.
This wild, ungoverned growth, this worthless, thick,
And unsuppressible fecundity
Was dotted with a scattering of graves
Of the most modest sort: worn, simple stones
From which all carving had been long effaced,
And under which the mute, anonymous dead
Slept in supreme indifference to the green
Havoc about them, the discourse of guides,
The bewildered tourists, acres of desolation.

Marriages come to grief in many ways.
Our own was, I suppose, a common one,
Without dramatics, a slow stiffening
Of all the little signs of tenderness,
Significant silences, self-conscious efforts
To be civil even when we were alone.
The cause may be too deep ever to find,
And I have long since ceased all inquiry.
It seems to me in fact that Martha and I
Were somehow victims of a nameless blight
And dark interior illness. We were both
Decent and well-intentioned, capable
Of love and devotion and all the rest of it,
Had it not been for what in other ages
Might have been thought of as the wrath of God,
The cold, envenoming spirit of Despair,
Turning what was the nectar of the world
To ashes in our mouths. We were the cursed
To whom it seemed no joy was possible,
The spiritually warped and handicapped.
It seems, in retrospect, as I look over
The pages of this journal, that the moments
Of what had once seemed love were an illusion,
The agreement, upon instinct, of two people
Grandly to overestimate each other,
An accord essentially self-flattering,
The paradise of fools before the fall.
What sticks in the mind, what I cannot escape,
Is the setting in which we found ourselves that day
I first began to see us as outcast:
The ugliness of the landscape, the conviction
That no painter would think it worth a glance.

There are both places and periods in life
That are tolerable only as transitions;
Hell might consist in staying there forever,
Immobile, never able to depart.
Such was the vision I received that day,
Raised, as it chanced, to perhaps the ultimate power
By reading the letters of the Younger Pliny.
His distinguished uncle, the revered old man,
Author of the great *Natural History*
In thirty-seven volumes, was stationed here
On this promontory, just where I had been,
At the time disaster struck. There had been flames
And leaping fires made the more terrible
By the darkness of the night. He was a stout man,
And, from the fumes and smoke, found it hard to breathe.
But he had tied a pillow over his head
As protection against falling rocks and pumice,
And calmly went about to satisfy
His scientific curiosity.
Of all those strange sights the most ominous
Was perhaps the sudden vision of the sea
Sucked out and drained away by the earthquake
That was part of the eruption, leaving a sea-bed
Of naked horrors lighted now and then
By jets of fire and sheet-lightning flares,
Only to be folded back into the dark.
One could make out in such brief intervals
An endless beach littered with squirming fish,
With kelp and timbers strewn on muddy flats,
Giant sea-worms bright with a glittering slime,
Crabs limping in their rheumatoid pavane.

CROWS IN WINTER

Here's a meeting
of morticians in our trees.
They agree in klaxon voices:
things are looking good.
The snowfields signify
a landscape of clean skulls,
Seas of Tranquillity
throughout the neighborhood.

Here's a mined,
a graven wisdom,
a bituminous air.
The first cosmetic pinks
of dawn amuse them greatly.

They foresee the expansion of graveyards,
they talk real estate.
Cras, they say,
repeating a rumor
among the whitened branches.

And the wind, a voiceless thorn,
goes over the details,
making a soft promise
to take our breath away.

THE TRANSPARENT MAN

I'm mighty glad to see you, Mrs. Curtis,
And thank you very kindly for this visit—
Especially now when all the others here
Are having holiday visitors, and I feel
A little conspicuous and in the way.
It's mainly because of Thanksgiving. All these mothers
And wives and husbands gaze at me soulfully
And feel they should break up their box of chocolates
For a donation, or hand me a chunk of fruitcake.
What they don't understand and never guess
Is that it's better for me without a family;
It's a great blessing. Though I mean no harm.
And as for visitors, why, I have you,
All cheerful, brisk and punctual every Sunday,
Like church, even if the aisles smell of phenol.
And you always bring even better gifts than any
On your book-trolley. Though they mean only good,
Families can become a sort of burden.
I've only got my father, and he won't come,
Poor man, because it would be too much for him.
And for me, too, so it's best the way it is.
He knows, you see, that I will predecease him,
Which is hard enough. It would take a callous man
To come and stand around and watch me failing.
(Now don't you fuss; we both know the plain facts.)
But for him it's even harder. He loved my mother.
They say she looked like me; I suppose she may have.
Or rather, as I grew older I came to look
More and more like she must one time have looked,
And so the prospect for my father now
Of losing me is like having to lose her twice.
I know he frets about me. Dr. Frazer
Tells me he phones in every single day,
Hoping that things will take a turn for the better.
But with leukemia things don't improve.

It's like a sort of blizzard in the bloodstream,
A deep, severe, unseasonable winter,
Burying everything. The white blood cells
Multiply crazily and storm around,
Out of control. The chemotherapy
Hasn't helped much, and it makes my hair fall out.
I know I look a sight, but I don't care.
I care about fewer things; I'm more selective.
It's got so I can't even bring myself
To read through any of your books these days.
It's partly weariness, and partly the fact
That I seem not to care much about the endings,
How things work out, or whether they even do.
What I do instead is sit here by this window
And look out at the trees across the way.
You wouldn't think that was much, but let me tell you,
It keeps me quite intent and occupied.
Now all the leaves are down, you can see the spare,
Delicate structures of the sycamores,
The fine articulation of the beeches.
I have sat here for days studying them,
And I have only just begun to see
What it is that they resemble. One by one,
They stand there like magnificent enlargements
Of the vascular system of the human brain.
I see them there like huge discarnate minds,
Lost in their meditative silences.
The trunks, branches and twigs compose the vessels
That feed and nourish vast immortal thoughts.
So I've assigned them names. There, near the path,
Is the great brain of Beethoven, and Kepler
Haunts the wide spaces of that mountain ash.
This view, you see, has become my Hall of Fame.
It came to me one day when I remembered
Mary Beth Finley who used to play with me

When we were girls. One year her parents gave her
A birthday toy called "The Transparent Man."
It was made of plastic, with different colored organs,
And the circulatory system all mapped out
In rivers of red and blue. She'd asked me over
And the two of us would sit and study him
Together, and do a powerful lot of giggling.
I figure he's most likely the only man
Either of us would ever get to know
Intimately, because Mary Beth became
A Sister of Mercy when she was old enough.
She must be thirty-one; she was a year
Older than I, and about four inches taller.
I used to envy both those advantages
Back in those days. Anyway, I was struck
Right from the start by the sea-weed intricacy,
The fine-haired, silken-threaded filiations
That wove, like Belgian lace, throughout the head.
But this last week it seems I have found myself
Looking beyond, or through, individual trees
At the dense, clustered woodland just behind them,
Where those great, nameless crowds patiently stand.
It's become a sort of complex, ultimate puzzle
And keeps me fascinated. My eyes are twenty-twenty,
Or used to be, but of course I can't unravel
The tousled snarl of intersecting limbs,
That mackled, cinder greyness. It's a riddle
Beyond the eye's solution. Impenetrable.
If there is order in all that anarchy
Of granite mezzotint, that wilderness,
It takes a better eye than mine to see it.
It set me on to wondering how to deal
With such a thickness of particulars,
Deal with it faithfully, you understand,
Without blurring the issue. Of course I know
That within a month the sleeving snows will come
With cold, selective emphases, with massings

And arbitrary contrasts, rendering things
Deceptively simple, thickening the twigs
To frosty veins, bestowing epaulets
And decorations on every birch and aspen.
And the eye, self-satisfied, will be misled,
Thinking the puzzle solved, supposing at last
It can look forth and comprehend the world.
That's when you have to really watch yourself.
So I hope that you won't think me plain ungrateful
For not selecting one of your fine books,
And I take it very kindly that you came
And sat here and let me rattle on this way.

THE BOOK OF YOLEK

Wir haben ein Gesetz,
Und nach dem Gesetz soll er sterben.

The dowsed coals fume and hiss after your meal
Of grilled brook trout, and you saunter off for a walk
Down the fern trail, it doesn't matter where to,
Just so you're weeks and worlds away from home,
And among midsummer hills have set up camp
In the deep bronze glories of declining day.

You remember, peacefully, an earlier day
In childhood, remember a quite specific meal:
A corn roast and bonfire in summer camp.
That summer you got lost on a Nature Walk;
More than you dared admit, you thought of home;
No one else knows where the mind wanders to.

The fifth of August, 1942.
It was morning and very hot. It was the day
They came at dawn with rifles to The Home
For Jewish Children, cutting short the meal
Of bread and soup, lining them up to walk
In close formation off to a special camp.

How often you have thought about that camp,
As though in some strange way you were driven to,
And about the children, and how they were made to walk,
Yolek who had bad lungs, who wasn't a day
Over five years old, commanded to leave his meal
And shamble between armed guards to his long home.

We're approaching August again. It will drive home
The regulation torments of that camp
Yolek was sent to, his small, unfinished meal,
The electric fences, the numeral tattoo,
The quite extraordinary heat of the day
They all were forced to take that terrible walk.

Whether on a silent, solitary walk
Or among crowds, far off or safe at home,
You will remember, helplessly, that day,
And the smell of smoke, and the loudspeakers of the camp.
Wherever you are, Yolek will be there, too.
His unuttered name will interrupt your meal.

Prepare to receive him in your home some day.
Though they killed him in the camp they sent him to,
He will walk in as you're sitting down to a meal.

from FLIGHT AMONG THE TOMBS

from THE PRESUMPTIONS OF ÐEATH

Woodcuts by Leonard Baskin

DEATH SAUNTERING ABOUT

The crowds have gathered here by the paddock gates
And racing silks like the flags of foreign states
 Billow and snap in the sun,
And thoroughbreds prance and paw the turf, the race
Is hotly contested, for win and show and place,
 Before it has yet begun.

The ladies' gowns in corals and mauves and reds,
Like fluently changing variegated beds
 Of a wild informal garden,
Float hither and yon where gentlemen advance
Questions of form, the inscrutable ways of chance,
 As edges of shadow harden.

Among these holiday throngs, a passer-by,
Mute, unremarked, insouciant, saunter I,
 One who has placed—
Despite the tumult, the pounding of hooves, the sweat,
And the urgent importance of everybody's bet—
 No premium on haste.

DEATH THE ARCHBISHOP

... and the almond tree shall flourish, and the
grasshopper shall be a burden, and desire shall
fail; because man goeth to his long home; and
the mourners go about the streets.

Ah my poor erring flock,
Truant and slow to come unto my ways,
    Making an airy mock
Of those choice pastures where my chosen graze,
You loiter childishly in pleasure's maze,
    Unheedful of the clock.

    Mere tuneless vanities
Deflect you from the music of my word;
    You haste or take your ease
As if your cadences could be deferred,
Giving your whole consent to brief, absurd
    And piping symphonies.

    The crozier, alb and cope
Compose the ancient blazons of my truth
    Whose broad intent and scope
Shows how discordant are the glees of youth,
How weak the serum of that serpent's tooth
    The ignorant call *Hope.*

    Yet shall you come to see
In articles and emblems of my faith
    That in mortality
Lies all our comfort, as the preacher saith,
And to the blessèd kingdom of the wraith
    I have been given the key.

A Ballade-Lament for the Makers

Where have they gone, the lordly makers,
Torchlight and fire-folk of our skies,
Those grand authorial earthshakers
Who brought such gladness to the eyes
Of the knowing and unworldly-wise
In damasked language long ago?
Call them and nobody replies.
Et nunc in pulvere dormio.

The softly spoken verbal Quakers
Who made no fuss and told no lies;
Baroque and intricate risk-takers,
Full of elliptical surprise
From Mother Goose to Paradise
Lost and Regained, where did they go?
This living hand indites, and dies,
Et nunc in pulvere dormio.

Old Masters, thunderous as the breakers
Tennyson's eloquence defies,
Beneath uncultivated acres
Our great original, Shakespeare, lies
With Grub Street hacks he would despise,
Quelled by the common ratio
That cuts all scribblers down to size,
Et nunc in pulvere dormio.

Archduke of Darkness, who supplies
The deadline governing joy and woe,
Here I put off my flesh disguise
Et nunc in pulvere dormio.

DEATH THE PAINTER

Snub-nosed, bone-fingered, deft with engraving tools,
    I have alone been given
The powers of Joshua, who stayed the sun
    In its traverse of heaven.
Here in this Gotham of unnumbered fools
I have sought out and arrested everyone.

Under my watchful eye all human creatures
    Convert to a *still life,*
As with unique precision I apply
    White lead and palette knife.
A model student of remodelled features,
The final barber, the last beautician, I.

You lordlings, what is Man, his blood and vitals,
    When all is said and done?
A poor forked animal, a nest of flies.
    Tell us, what is this one
Once shorn of all his dignities and titles,
Divested of his testicles and eyes?

DEATH THE WHORE

I

Some thin grey smoke twists up against a sky
Of German silver in the sullen dusk
From a small chimney among leafless trees.
The paths are empty, the weeds bent and dead;
Winter has taken hold. And what, my dear,
Does this remind you of? You are surprised
By the familiar manner, the easy, sure
Intimacy of my address. You wonder,
Whose curious voice is this? Why should that scene
Seem distantly familiar? Did something happen
Back in my youth on a deserted path
Late on some unremembered afternoon?
And now you'll feel at times a fretful nagging
At the back of your mind as of something almost grasped
But tauntingly and cunningly evasive.
It may go on for months, perhaps for years.
Think of the memory game that children played
So long ago. A grown-up brought a tray
Laden with objects hidden by a shawl
Or coverlet with fine brocaded flowers
Beneath which, like the roofs of a small city,
Some secret things lay cloaked. Then at a signal
The cloth was whisked away for thirty seconds.
You were allowed to do nothing but look,
And then the cover was replaced. Remember?
The tray contained bright densely crowded objects,
Sometimes exotic—a small cloisonné egg,
A candle-snuffer with an ivory handle—
But simple things as well. It never occurred
To any of the children there to count them;

You had been told simply to memorize
The contents of the tray. Each child was given
Paper and pencil to list what he recalled
And no one ever finally got them all;
Something always escaped. Perhaps a needle,
A gum eraser or a plastic ruler.
And so it is that now, as you're about
To eat or light a cigarette, something
Passes too swiftly before you can take aim,
Passes in furtive silence, in disguise,
Glimpsed only hazily in retrospect—
Like a clock's strokes recounted once they're done,
Never with confidence.
                                    And now you're angry
At what you think of as my long digression
When in fact it's the eclipses of your mind,
Those sink-holes, culverts, cisterns long avoided
As dangerous, where the actual answer lies.
As for my indirection, I'll just say
I have more time than I know what to do with.
Let me give you a hint. The voice you hear
Is not the voice of someone you remember—
Or rather, it's that voice now greatly altered
By certain events of which you've partly heard,
Partly imagined, altogether feared.
Does that help? No, I didn't think it would.
Perhaps we can return another time
(A time when you're conveniently abstracted)
To the topic of my voice and of that smoke.

II

Much time elapses. (I could count the days;
You, for your part, have no idea how many.)
Today a color ad for undergarments,
Some glossy pages of *Victoria's Secret*,
Modelled by a young blonde catches your eye.
Nothing so vivid as a memory
Results. Perhaps a vague erotic sense,
A fleeting impulse down between your legs,
Stirs like a sleeping dog. Your mind begins
Its little, paltry Leporello's list
Of former girlfriends who pass in review
As images, stripped even of their names.
And then you linger upon one. It's me.
Don't be surprised. All that was long ago.
Your indolent thought goes over my young breasts,
Remembering, fondling, exciting you.
How very long ago that was. It lasted
Almost two years. Two mainly happy years.
In all that time, what did you learn of me?
My name, my body, how best to go about
Mutual arousal, my taste in food and drink
And what would later be called "substances."
(These days among my friends I might be called
"A woman of substance" if I were still around.)
You also learned, from a casual admission,
That I had twice attempted suicide.
Tact on both sides had left this unexplored.
We both seemed to like sex for the same reason.

It was, as they used to say, a "little death,"
A tiny interval devoid of thought
When even sensation is so localized
Only one part of the body seems alive.
And when you left I began the downhill slope.
First one-night stands; then quickly I turned pro
In order to get all the drugs I wanted.
My looks went fast. I didn't really care.
The thing that I'd been after from the first,
With you, with sex, with drugs, was oblivion.
So it was easy. A simple overdose
Knocked back with half a bottle of good Scotch.
In later years the rumors found you out
Through mutual friends. And somehow you remembered
That I had been disowned by my family.
My parents would have nothing to do with me
After they found I'd been a prostitute,
To say nothing of my trial suicides.
So, as you guessed, when I at last succeeded,
They acted as if I never had been born.
("Let the day perish . . . ," as the scripture says.)
There was no funeral, no cemetery,
Nowhere for you to come in pilgrimage—
Although from time to time you thought of me.
Oh yes, my dear, you thought of me; I know.
But less and less, of course, as time went on.
And then you learned by a chance word of mouth
That I had been cremated, thereby finding
More of oblivion than I'd even hoped for.

And now when I occur to you, the voice
You hear is not the voice of what I was
When young and sexy and perhaps in love,
But the weary voice shaped in your later mind
By a small sediment of fact and rumor,
A faceless voice, a voice without a body.

As for the winter scene of which I spoke—
The smoke, my dear, the smoke. I am the smoke.

DEATH THE FILM DIRECTOR

Open with a long shot. Chimneys and spires
Of the old town, rouged in the copper glow
Of sunset. Intense, arterial red
Dyeing the trees as day slowly expires,
Staining the churches, pathways, fence posts, spread
From roof to roof, while, rising from below,
Cool tides of shadow lap the countryside,

Engulf the cemetery headstones, shroud
Arbor, toolshed, curbstone and portico.
Now from behind a lazily drifting cloud
A full, Pierrot-white moon; its bleaching light
Drains the lifeblood of everything in sight.
Zoom down to a derelict alley, a scrawny cat
Sniffing through toppled garbage till it finds
A male, black-skinned, mature, immobile hand,
Its parent limb, head, body, all concealed
By liquor cartons, broken Venetian blinds,
Worn tires, an unravelled welcome mat.
The creature paws at a finger, which remains
Inert, sniffs once again, looks up and walks
Calmly across the hand into the dark.
Credits. The title, the studio, the stars
Flash on, then fade. Henry Mancini noise.
And then my name glows on the darkened screen.
It lingers there a while, etching the mind
Of every member of the audience.
As well it should. This film required of me
Immense executive abilities—
All those subordinates to keep in line,
Trained to alert me with their signal cries:
"Ready when *you* are, C.B." That's what I like,
That fine docility. As for the cast,
If the truth be known, actors are idiots.
Theirs is the glamour, of course. Their gorgeous looks,
Along with large, unmerited salaries,
Must compensate them for their tiny minds.
But in the end, after repeated takes,
The prints, the cutting-room floor, I am the one
Who sees that everything falls into place,
The master plan. This film has a large cast,
A huge cast; countless, you might almost say;
And for them all, for every one of them,
I have designed, with supreme artfulness,
What could be called an inevitable plot.

DEATH THE CARNIVAL BARKER

con brio

Step forward, please! Make room for those in back!
Come in and see the greatest show on earth!
I promise it will take your breath away!
Something you're sure to call your money's worth;
And bound to last forever and a day!
Softer than down; more powerful than crack!

Flame-eaters, jugglers, the two-headed boy
Are merely trifles by comparison.
We've got the ultimate show to freak you out.
The surest cure for worry under the sun—
As well as toothache, blindness, debt and gout.
There's nothing that you'll ever more enjoy!

The little lady with the long blonde hair
Will issue you a ticket for the price
Of your life savings, your miserable estate,
The shirt right off your back. Take my advice:
It's the best deal you'll ever get. Why wait?
We're known throughout the world as fair and square.

And talk of fairness! Talk of equality!
Give me your poor, your homeless. I admit
The halt, the deaf, all races and all trades.
O you rejected ones, unwashed, unfit,
Entrust yourselves to the keeping of my aids.
No quota, bribe, initiation fee!

No one has ever asked for his money back!
Geniuses, beauties, all the greatest wits
Have been our patrons! Once the show's begun
Small kids admitted for a mere two-bits!
Fear not, my friends! There's room for everyone!
Step forward, please! Make room for those in back!

———

THE WHIRLIGIG OF TIME

HORACE I:25

They are fewer these days, those supple, suntanned boys
Whose pebbles tapped at your window, and your door
Swings less and less on its obliging hinges
For wildly importunate suitors. Fewer the cries
Of "Lydia, how can you sleep when I've got the hots?
I won't last out the night; let me get my rocks off."
Things have moved right along, and, behold, it's you
Who quails, like a shrivelled whore, as they scorn and dodge you,
And the wind shrieks like a sex-starved thing in heat
As the moon goes dark and the mouth of your old dry vulva
Rages and hungers, and your worst, most ulcerous pain
Is knowing those sleek-limbed boys prefer the myrtle,
The darling buds of May, leaving dried leaves
To cluster in unswept corners, fouling doorways.

PROSPECTS

We have set out from here for the sublime
Pastures of summer shade and mountain stream;
I have no doubt we shall arrive on time.

Is all the green of that enamelled prime
A snapshot recollection or a dream?
We have set out from here for the sublime

Without provisions, without one thin dime,
And yet, for all our clumsiness, I deem
It certain that we shall arrive on time.

No guidebook tells you if you'll have to climb
Or swim. However foolish we may seem,
We have set out from here for the sublime

And must get past the scene of an old crime
Before we falter and run out of steam,
Riddled by doubt that we'll arrive on time.

Yet even in winter a pale paradigm
Of birdsong utters its obsessive theme.
We have set out from here for the sublime;
I have no doubt we shall arrive on time.

LÀ-BAS: A TRANCE

From silk route Samarkand, emeralds and drugs
Find their way west, smuggled by leather-capped
Bandits with lard-greased hair across unmapped
Storm-tossed sand oceans drained to the very dregs,

And thence to such ports of call as Amsterdam,
The waters of its intricate canals
Gold-leafed and amethyst-shadowed by the veils
Of cloud-occluded suns, imaged in dim

Hempen mirages and opium reveries
Crowding the mind of a Parisian poet
With jasmine adornments to his barren garret,
The masts of frigates from all seven seas

Moored just outside his window, their bright rigging
What all his neighbors know as laundry lines.
France is as nothing; France and her finest wines
For all this fellow's interest can go begging

As the doors of his perception open wide
Admitting nothing but those nacreous errors
Harvested from unfathomed depths of mirrors:
Harems of young, voluptuous, sloe-eyed

Houris, undressed, awaiting his commands,
Untiring courtyard fountains casting jewels
Thriftlessly into blue-and-white-tiled pools,
Their splashes mingled with languid sarabandes.

Carpaccio's Middle East evokes an air-borne
Carpet, a sash and headgear the color of flame
Turned into Holland's tulips whose very name
Comes to him from the Turkish word for turban.

MATISSE: BLUE INTERIOR WITH TWO GIRLS—1947

. . . he lived through some of the most traumatic political events
of recorded history, the worst wars, the greatest slaughters, the
most demented rivalries of ideology, without, it seems, turning a
hair. . . . Perhaps Matisse did suffer from fear and loathing
like the rest of us, but there is no trace of them in his work. His
studio was a world within a world: a place of equilibrium
that, for sixty continuous years, produced images of comfort,
refuge, and balanced satisfaction.

      —ROBERT HUGHES, *The Shock of the New*

Outside is variable May, a lawn of immediate green,
   The tree as blue as its shadow.
      A shutter angles out in charitable shade.
It is a world of yearning: we yearn for it,
   Its youthful natives yearn for one another.
      Their flesh is firm as a plum, their smooth tanned waists,
Lit through the fluttered leaves above their heads,
   Are rubbed and cinctured with this morning's bangles.
      Yet each, if we but take thought, is a lean gnomon,
A bone finger with its moral point:
   The hour, the minute, the dissolving pleasure.
      (Light fails, the shadows pool themselves in hollows.)
Here, in the stifling fragrance of mock orange,
   In the casual glance, the bright lust of the eye,
      Lies the hot spring of inevitable tears.

Within is the cool blue perfect cube of thought.
   The branched spirea carefully arranged
      Is no longer random growth: it now becomes
The object of our thought, it becomes our thought.
   The room is a retreat in which the drone
      Of the electric fan is modest, unassertive,
Faithful, as with a promise of lemonade
   And other gentle solaces of summer,

Among which, for the two serene young girls
In this cool tank of blue, is an open book
Where they behold the pure unchanging text
Of manifold, reverberating depth,
Quiet and tearless in its permanence.
Deep in their contemplation the two girls,
Regarding art, have become art themselves.
Once out of nature, they have settled here
In this blue room of thought, beyond the reach
Of the small brief sad ambitions of the flesh.

PROUST ON SKATES

*He stayed in bed, and at the beginning of October still wasn't
getting up till two in the afternoon. But he made a seventy-mile
journey to Chamonix to join Albu* [Louis d'Albufera] *and
Louisa* [de Mornand, Albufera's beautiful mistress] *on
a mule-back excursion to Montanvert, where they went skating.*
—RONALD HAYMAN, *Proust: A Biography*

The alpine forests, like huddled throngs of mourners,
Black, hooded, silent, resign themselves to wait
    As long as may be required;
A low pneumonia mist covers the glaciers,
Spruces are bathed in a cold sweat, the late
    Sun has long since expired,

Though barely risen, and the grey cast of the day
Is stark, unsentimental, and metallic.
    Earth-stained and chimney-soiled
Snow upon path and post is here to stay,
Foundered in endless twilight, a poor relic
    Of a once gladder world.

Sparse café patrons can observe a few
Skaters skimming the polished soapstone lake,
    A platform for their skill
At crosscut, grapevine, loop and curlicue,
Engelmann's Star, embroideries that partake
    Of talent, coaching, drill,

While a few tandem lovers, hand in hand,
Perform their *pas de deux* along the edges,
    Oblivious, unconcerned.
This is a stony, vapor-haunted land
Of granite dusk, of wind sieved by the hedges,
    Their branches braced and thorned.

Escaped from the city's politics and fribble,
Hither has come an odd party of three,
    Braided by silken ties:
With holiday abandon, the young couple
Have retreated into the deep privacy
    Of one another's eyes,

While the third, who in different ways yet loves them both,
Finds himself now, as usual, all alone,
    And lacing on his skates,
Steadies himself, cautiously issues forth
Into the midst of strangers and his own
    Interior debates.

Sweatered and mufflered to protect the weak
And lacey branches of his bronchial tree
    From the fine-particled threat
Of the moist air, he curves in an oblique
And gentle gradient, floating swift and free—
    No *danseur noble*, and yet

He glides with a gaining confidence, inscribes
Tentative passages, thinks again, backtracks,
    Comes to a minute point,
Then wheels about in widening sweeps and lobes,
Large Palmer cursives and smooth *entrelacs*,
    Preoccupied, intent

On a subtle, long-drawn style and pliant script
Incised with twin steel blades and qualified
    Perfectly to express,
With arms flung wide or gloved hands firmly gripped
Behind his back, attentively, clear-eyed,
    A glancing happiness.

It will not last, that happiness; nothing lasts;
But will reduce in time to the clear brew
    Of simmering memory
Nourished by shadowy gardens, music, guests,
Childhood affections, and, of Delft, a view
    Steeped in a sip of tea.

from THE DARKNESS AND THE LIGHT

LATE AFTERNOON: THE ONSLAUGHT OF LOVE

At this time of day
One could hear the caulking irons sound
Against the hulls in the dockyard.
Tar smoke rose between trees
And large oily patches floated on the water,
Undulating unevenly
In the purple sunlight
Like the surfaces of Florentine bronze.

At this time of day
Sounds carried clearly
Through hot silences of fading daylight.
The weedy fields lay drowned
In odors of creosote and salt.
Richer than double-colored taffeta,
Oil floated in the harbor,
Amoeboid, iridescent, limp.
It called to mind the slender limbs
Of Donatello's *David*.

It was lovely and she was in love.
They had taken a covered boat to one of the islands.
The city sounds were faint in the distance:
Rattling of carriages, tumult of voices,
Yelping of dogs on the decks of barges.
At this time of day
Sunlight empurpled the world.
The poplars darkened in ranks
Like imperial servants.
Water lapped and lisped
In its native and quiet tongue.
Oakum was in the air and the scent of grasses.
There would be fried smelts and cherries and cream.
Nothing designed by Italian artisans
Would match this evening's perfection.
The puddled oil was a miracle of colors.

MIRROR

for J. D. McClatchy

Always halfway between you and your double,
Like Washington, I cannot tell a lie.
When the dark queen demands in her querulous treble,
"Who is the fairest?," inaudibly I reply,

"Beauty, your highness, dwells in the clouded cornea
Of the self-deceived beholder, whereas Truth,
According to film moguls of California,
Lies in makeup, smoke and mirrors, gin and vermouth,

Or the vinous second-pressings of *Veritas,*
Much swilled at Harvard. The astronomer's speculum
Reveals it, and to the politician's cheval glass
It's that part of a horse he cannot distinguish from

His elbow; but it's also the upside-down
Melodies of Bach fugues, the right-to-left
Writing of Leonardo, a long-term loan
From Hebrew, retrograde fluencies in deft,

Articulate penmanship. An occasional Louis
Might encounter it in the corridors of Versailles;
It evades the geometrician's confident QE
D, but the constant motion from ground to sky

And back again of the terrible Ferris wheel
Sackville describes in *A Mirror for Magistrates*
Conveys some semblance of the frightening feel
Of the mechanical heartlessness of Fate,

The ring-a-ding-*Ding-an-Sich*. Yet think how gaily
In the warped fun-house glass our flesh dissolves
In shape and helpless laughter, unlike the Daily
Mirror in which New Yorkers saw themselves.

It's when no one's around that I'm most truthful,
In a world as timeless as before The Fall.
No one to reassure that she's still youthful,
I gaze untroubled at the opposite wall.

Light fades, of course, with the oncoming of dusk;
I faithfully note the rheostat dial of day
That will rise to brilliance, weaken as it must
Through each uncalibrated shade of grey,

One of them that of winter afternoons,
Desolate, leaden, and in its burden far
Deeper than darkness, engrossing in its tones
Those shrouded regions where the meanings are."

A FALL

Those desolate, brute, chilling sublimities,
Unchanging but as the light may chance to fall,
Deserts of snow, forlorn barrens of rock,
What could be more indifferent to man's life
Than your average Alp, stripped to the blackened bone
Above the tree line, except where the ice rags,
Patches, and sheets of winter cling yearlong?
The cowbell's ludicrous music, the austere
Sobrieties of Calvin, precision watches,
A cheese or two, and that is all the Swiss
Have given the world, unless we were to cite
The questionable morals of their banks.
But how are people to live in dignity
When at two p.m. the first shadows of night,
Formed by the massive shoulder of some slope,
Cast, for the rest of the day, entire valleys—
Their window boxes of geraniums,
Their cobbles, pinecones, banners and coffee cups—
Into increasing sinks and pools of dark?
And that is but half the story. The opposing slope
Keeps morning from its flaxen charities
Until, on midsummer days, eleven-thirty,
When fresh birdsong and cow dung rinse the air
And all outdoors still glistens with night-dew.
All this serves to promote a state of mind
Cheerless and without prospects. But yesterday
I let myself, in spite of dark misgivings,
Be talked into a strenuous excursion
Along one high ridge promising a view.

And suddenly, at a narrowing of the path,
The whole earth fell away, and dizzily
I beheld the most majestic torrent in Europe,
A pure cascade, over six hundred feet,
Falling straight down—it was like Rapunzel's hair,
But white, as if old age and disappointment
Had left her bereft of suitors. Down it plunged,
Its great, continuous, unending weight
Toppling from above in a long shaft
Or carven stem that broke up at its base
Into enormous rhododendron blooms
Of spray, a dense array of shaken blossoms.
I teetered perilously, scared and dazed,
And slowly, careful of both hand and foot,
Made my painstaking way back down the trail.
That evening in my bedroom I recalled
The scene's terror and grandeur, my vertigo
Mixed with a feeling little short of awe.
And I retraced my steps in the secure
Comfort of lamplight on a Baedeker.
That towering waterfall I just had viewed
At what had seemed the peril of my life
Was regarded locally with humorous
Contempt, and designated the *Pisse-Vache*.

Etched on the window were barbarous thistles of frost,
Edged everywhere in that tame winter sunlight
With pavé diamonds and fine prickles of ice
Through which a shaft of the late afternoon
Entered our room to entertain the sway
And float of motes, like tiny aqueous lives,
Then glanced off the silver teapot, raising stains
Of snailing gold upcast across the ceiling,
And bathed itself at last in the slop bucket
Where other aqueous lives, equally slow,
Turned in their sad, involuntary courses,
Swiveled in eel-green broth. Who could have known
Of any elsewhere? Even of out-of-doors,
Where the stacked firewood gleamed in drapes of glaze
And blinded the sun itself with jubilant theft,
The smooth cool plunder of celestial fire?

SAUL AND DAVID

It was a villainous spirit, snub-nosed, foul
Of breath, thick-taloned and malevolent,
That squatted within him wheresoever he went
    And possessed the soul of Saul.

There was no peace on pillow or on throne.
In dreams the toothless, dwarfed, and squinny-eyed
Started a joyful rumor that he had died
    Unfriended and alone.

The doctors were confounded. In his distress, he
Put aside arrogant ways and condescended
To seek among the flocks where they were tended
    By the youngest son of Jesse,

A shepherd boy, but goodly to look upon,
Unnoticed but God-favored, sturdy of limb
As Michelangelo later imagined him,
    Comely even in his frown.

Shall a mere shepherd provide the cure of kings?
Heaven itself delights in ironies such
As this, in which a boy's fingers would touch
    Pythagorean strings

And by a modal artistry assemble
The very Sons of Morning, the ranked and choired
Heavens in sweet laudation of the Lord,
    And make Saul cease to tremble.

DESPAIR

Sadness. The moist grey shawls of drifting sea-fog,
Salting scrub pine, drenching the cranberry bogs,
Erasing all but foreground, making a ghost
Of anyone who walks softly away;
And the faint, penitent psalmody of the ocean.

Gloom. It appears among the winter mountains
On rainy days. Or the tiled walls of the subway
In caged and aging light, in the steel scream
And echoing vault of the departing train,
The vacant platform, the yellow destitute silence.

But despair is another matter. Mid-afternoon
Washes the worn bank of a dry arroyo,
Its ocher crevices, unrelieved rusts,
Where a startled lizard pauses, nervous, exposed
To the full glare of relentless marigold sunshine.

JUDITH

It took less valor than I'm reputed for.
Since I was a small child I have hated men.
Even the feeblest, in their fantasies,
Triumph as sexual athletes, putting the shot
Squarely between the thighs of some meek woman,
While others strut like decathlon champions,
Like royal David hankering after his neighbor's
Dutiful wife. For myself, I found a husband
Not very prepossessing, but very rich.
Neither of us was interested in children.
In my case, the roving hands, the hot tumescence of an uncle,
Weakened my taste for close intimacies.
Ironically, heaven had granted me
What others took to be attractive features
And an alluring body, and which for years
Instinctively I looked upon with shame.
All men seemed stupid in their lecherous,
Self-flattering appetites, which I found repugnant.
But at last, as fate would have it, I found a chance
To put my curse to practical advantage.
It was easy. Holofernes was pretty tight;
I had only to show some cleavage and he was done for.

LOOK DEEP

Look deep into my eyes. Think to yourself,
"There is 'the fringèd curtain' where a play
Will shortly be enacted." Look deep down
Into the pupil. Think, "I am going to sleep."

The pupil has its many-tinctured curtain
Of moiré silks, parted to let you in,
And the play will present a goddess you used to know
From the glint of sunlit fountain, from bevelled mirror,

A goddess, yes, but only a messenger
Whose message is the armorial fleur-de-lys
She carries in her right hand, signifying
The majesty of France, as handed down

From the royal house of Solomon and David:
Wisdom, music and valor gracefully joined
In trefoil heraldry. Nearly asleep,
You settle down for a full-scale production

Of *The Rainstorm* in its grand entirety,
Which, greater than *The Ring*, lasts forty nights;
Everything huddled in one rocking stateroom,
A saving remnant, a life-raft-world in little.

Dream at your ease of the dark forests of spruce
Swaying in currents of green, gelatinous winds
Above which the classless zoo and zookeepers
Weather the testing and baptismal waters;

Dream of the long, undeviating gloom,
The unrelenting skies, the pounding wet
Through which a peak will thrust, a light, and over
The covenanted ark, an *arc-en-ciel*.

SACRIFICE

I   ABRAHAM

Long years, and I found favor
In the sight of the Lord, who brought me out of Ur
To where his promise lay,
There with him to confer
On Justice and Mercy and the appointed day
Of Sodom's ashen fate;
For me he closeted sweetness in the date,
And gave to salt its savor.

Three promises he gave,
Came like three kings or angels to my door:
His purposes concealed
In coiled and kerneled store
He planted as a seedling that would yield
In my enfeebled years
A miracle that would command my tears
With piercings of the grave.

"Old man, behold Creation,"
Said the Lord, "the leaping hills, the thousand-starred
Heavens and watery floor.
Is anything too hard
For the Lord, who shut all seas within their doors?"
And then, for his name's sake
He led me, knowing where my heart would break,
Into temptation.

The whole of my long life
Pivoted on one terrible day at dawn.
Isaac, my son, and I
Were to Moriah gone.
There followed an hour in which I wished to die,
Being visited by these things:
My name called out, the beat of gigantic wings,
Faggots, and flame, and knife.

II ISAAC

Youthful I was and trusting and strong of limb,
The fresh-split firewood roped tight to my back,
And I bore unknowing that morning my funeral pyre.
My father, face averted, carried the flame,
And, in its scabbard, the ritual blade he bore.
It seemed to me at the time a wearisome trek.

I thought of my mother, how, in her age, the Lord
Had blessed her among women, giving her me
As joke and token both, unlikelihood
Being his way. But where, where from our herd
Was the sacrifice, I asked my father. He,
In a spasm of agony, bound me hand and foot.

I thought, *I am poured out like water, like wax*
My heart is melted in the midst of my bowels.
Both were tear-blinded. Hate and love and fear
Wrestled to ruin us, savage us beyond cure.
And the fine blade gleamed with the fury of live coals
Where we had reared an altar among the rocks.

Peace be to us both, to father Abraham,
To me, elected the shorn stunned lamb of God—
We were sentenced and reprieved by the same Voice—
And to all our seed, by this terror sanctified,
To be numbered even as the stars at the small price
Of an old scapegoated and thicket-baffled ram.

III 1945

It was widely known that the army of occupation
Was in full retreat. The small provincial roads
Rumbled now every night with tanks and trucks,
Echoed with cries in German, much *mach schnell,*
Zurück, ganz richtig, augenblicklich, jawohl,
Audible in the Normandy countryside.
So it had been for days, or, rather, nights,

The troops at first making their moves in darkness,
But pressures of haste toward the end of March
Left stragglers to make their single ways alone,
At their own risk, and even in daylight hours.

Since the soldiers were commandeering anything
They needed—food, drink, vehicles of all sorts—
One rural family dismantled their bicycle,
Daubed the chrome parts—rims, sprocket, spokes—with mud,
And wired them carefully to the upper boughs
Of the orchard. And the inevitable came
In the shape of a young soldier, weighted down
With pack and bedroll, rifle, entrenching tools,
Steel helmet and heavy boots just after dawn.
The family was at breakfast. He ordered them out
In front of the house with abusive German words
They couldn't understand, but gesture and rifle
Made his imperious wishes perfectly clear.
They stood in a huddled group, all nine of them.
And then he barked his furious command:
Fahrrad! They all looked blank. He shouted again:
FAHRRAD! FAHRRAD! FAHRRAD!, as though sheer volume
Joined with his anger would make his meaning plain.
The father of the family experimentally
Inquired, *Manger?* The soldier, furious,
At last dredged up an explosive *Bicyclette,*
Proud of himself, contemptuous of them.
To this the father in a small pantomime—
Shrugged shoulders, palms turned out, a helpless, long,
Slow shaking of the head, then the wide gesture
Of an arm, taking in all his property—
Conveyed *Nous n'avons pas de bicyclettes*
More clearly than his words. To the young soldier
This seemed unlikely. No one could live this far
From neighbors, on a poor untravelled road
That lacked phone lines, without the usual means
Of transport. There was no time to search

The house, the barn, cowsheds, coops, pens and grounds.
He looked at the frightened family huddled together,
And with the blunt nose of his rifle barrel
Judiciously singled out the eldest son,
A boy perhaps fourteen, but big for his years,
Obliging him to place himself alone
Against the whitewashed front wall of the house.
Then, at the infallible distance of ten feet,
With rifle pointed right at the boy's chest,
The soldier shouted what was certainly meant
To be his terminal order: *BICYCLETTE!*

It was still early on a chilly morning.
The water in the tire-treads of the road
Lay clouded, polished pale and chalked with frost,
Like the paraffin-sealed coverings of preserves.
The very grass was a stiff lead-crystal grey,
Though splendidly prismatic where the sun
Made its slow way between the lingering shadows
Of nearby fence posts and more distant trees.
There was leisure enough to take full note of this
In the most minute detail as the soldier held
Steady his index finger on the trigger.

It wasn't charity. Perhaps mere prudence,
Saving a valuable round of ammunition
For some more urgent crisis. Whatever it was,
The soldier reslung his rifle on his shoulder,
Turned wordlessly and walked on down the road
The departed German vehicles had taken.

There followed a long silence, a long silence.
For years they lived together in that house,
Through daily tasks, through all the family meals,
In agonized, unviolated silence.

THE ASHEN LIGHT OF DAWN

Reveille was bugled through army camps
As a soft dawn wind was fluttering street lamps.

It was that hour when smooth suntanned limbs
Of adolescents twitched with unlawful dreams,
When, like a bloodshot eye beside the bed,
A nightlamp soaked oncoming day in red,
When, weighted beneath a humid body's brawn,
The soul mimicked that duel of lamp and dawn.
Like a face dried by the wind of recent tears,
The air is rife with whatever disappears,
And woman wearies of love, man of his chores.

Here and there chimneys smoked. The local whores,
Mascara'ed, overpainted, slept a stone
And stupid sleep, while the impoverished crone,
Breasts limp and frigid, alternately blew
On embers and on fingers, both going blue.
It was the hour of grief, of chill, of want;
Women in childbirth felt their seizures mount;
Like a thick, blood-choked scream, a rooster crowed
Distantly from some dim, befogged abode
As a sea of fog engulfed the city blocks,
And in some seedy hospice, human wrecks
Breathed their death-rattling last, while debauchees
Tottered toward home, drained of their powers to please.

All pink and green in flounces, Aurora strolled
The vacant Seine embankments as the old,
Stupefied, blear-eyed Paris, glum and resigned,
Laid out his tools to begin the daily grind.

                    BAUDELAIRE

THE ROAD TO DAMASCUS

What happened? At first there were strange, confused accounts.
This man, said one, who had long for righteousness' sake
Delivered unto the death both men and women
In his zeal for the Lord, had tumbled from his mount,
Felled by an unheard Word and worded omen.
Another claimed his horse shied at a snake.

Yet a third, that he was convulsed by the onslaught
Of the falling sickness, whose victims we were urged
To spit upon as protection and in disgust.
Rigid in body now as in doctrine, caught
In a seizure known but to few, he lay in the dust,
Of all his fiercest resolves stunningly purged.

We are told by certain learned doctors that those
Thus stricken are granted an inkling of that state
Where *There Shall Be No More Time*, as it is said;
As though from a pail, spilled water were to repose
Mid-air in pebbles of clarity, all its weight
Turned light, in a glittering, loose, but stopped cascade.

The Damascene culprits now could rest untroubled,
Their delinquencies no longer the concern
Of this fallen, converted Pharisee. He rather
From sighted blindness to blind sight went hobbled
And was led forth to a house where he would turn
His wrath from one recusancy to another.

SARABANDE ON ATTAINING THE AGE
OF SEVENTY-SEVEN

The harbingers are come. See, see their mark;
White is their colour, and behold my head.

Long gone the smoke-and-pepper childhood smell
Of the smoldering immolation of the year,
Leaf-strewn in scattered grandeur where it fell,
Golden and poxed with frost, tarnished and sere.

And I myself have whitened in the weathers
Of heaped-up Januarys as they bequeath
The annual rings and wrongs that wring my withers,
Sober my thoughts and undermine my teeth.

The dramatis personae of our lives
Dwindle and wizen; familiar boyhood shames,
The tribulations one somehow survives,
Rise smokily from propitiatory flames

Of our forgetfulness until we find
It becomes strangely easy to forgive
Even ourselves with this clouding of the mind,
This cinerous blur and smudge in which we live.

A turn, a glide, a quarter-turn and bow,
The stately dance advances; these are airs
Bone-deep and numbing as I should know by now,
Diminishing the cast, like musical chairs.

"THE DARKNESS AND THE LIGHT
ARE BOTH ALIKE TO THEE"

PSALMS 139:12

Like trailing silks, the light
Hangs in the olive trees
As the pale wine of day
Drains to its very lees:
Huge presences of grey
Rise up, and then it's night.

Distantly lights go on.
Scattered like fallen sparks
Bedded in peat, they seem
Set in the plushest darks
Until a timid gleam
Of matins turns them wan,

Like the elderly and frail
Who've lasted through the night,
Cold brows and silent lips,
For whom the rising light
Entails their own eclipse,
Brightening as they fail.

Notes

Double Sonnet

3 *Pythagorean heavens:* Ancient Greek philosopher and mathematician Pythagoras (fl. sixth century B.C.) held that numbers were the ultimate reality, and that the heavens could be mathematically calculated in terms of patterns and cycles.

Japan

4 *atabrine:* Atabrine was the brand name of a quinine drug given to American troops in the Pacific during World War II to help prevent the onset of malaria. One of its side effects was to turn the skin yellowish.

5 *eye-born goddess:* In Japanese mythology, the sun goddess Amaterasu was born from the left eye of the god Izanagi.

5 *Schistosomiasis / Japonica:* A parasitic disease caused by the larvae of freshwater flatworms.

Samuel Sewall

7 *Samuel Sewall:* English-born American judge (1652–1730) who presided over the 1692 Salem witch trials.

A Poem for Julia

8 *Memling:* Flemish painter Hans Memling (c.1430–94). *Young Woman with a Pink,* now attributed to Memling, is in the Bache collection at the Metropolitan Museum in New York. The wimple and the landscape viewed through the window in the painting are invented by AH.

9 nulla est redemptio: Part of the Catholic Office of the Dead, in medieval Latin: *"Peccantem me quotidie, et non poenitentem, timor mortis conturbat me. Quia in inferno nulla est*

redemptio, miserere mei, Deus, et salva me." ("Sinning daily, and not repenting, the fear of death disturbs me. Because there is no redemption in hell, have mercy on me, O God, and save me.")

10 *the flourishing of the almond tree:* Ecclesiastes 12:5.

Christmas Is Coming

12 Christmas is coming. The goose is getting fat: A traditional nursery rhyme.

The Gardens of the Villa d'Este

14 *There is no garden:* The Villa d'Este is the magnificent sixteenth-century estate outside Rome commissioned by Cardinal Ippolito II d'Este, designed by Italian architect Pirro Ligorio (c.1510–83), and including terraced gardens and a sequence of cascading water fountains.

14 *Avogadro:* Italian physicist Amedeo Avogadro (1776–1856) hypothesized in 1811 that the number of molecules in a specific volume of gas is independent of their size or mass—a law since named after him.

14 *Hephaestus:* In Greek mythology, the lame god of fire and blacksmithing, who once used his net to capture his wife, Aphrodite, in the arms of her lover Ares.

15 *Brownian movement:* The random motion of particles in a fluid, a phenomenon named for Scottish botanist Robert Brown (1773–1858).

15 *Góngora:* Spanish baroque poet Luis de Góngora (1561–1627).

16 *Mozart's Figaro:* The wily servant Figaro is the title character in the 1786 opera *Le nozze di Figaro* (*The Marriage of Figaro*) by Austrian composer Wolfgang Amadeus Mozart (1756–91).

16 *Tartini:* Italian composer Giuseppe Tartini (1692–1770).

16 *the chaconne:* An eighteenth-century dance, slow and stately.

17 *Pliny's pregnant mouse:* In his *Natural History*, Roman naturalist Pliny the Elder (23–79) thought the mouse commonly so fertile that even its unborn might be pregnant.

Alceste in the Wilderness

19 Non, je ne puis souffrir: "No, I cannot bear so base a method, though most of society affects it . . . ," says Alceste in Act I of *Le Misanthrope* (*The Misanthrope*), the 1666 play by French playwright Jean-Baptiste Poquelin, known as Molière (1622–73). At the end of the play Alceste, despising society's hypocrisy in spite of his friend Philinte's more balanced views, resolves to retreat to the wilderness in order to escape the dishonesty of those around him.

19 *Daphnis:* A conventional Greek swain, here portrayed on a snuffbox.

19 *The small corpse of a monkey:* Compare the story of Samson in Judges, 14:5–20.

A Hill

23 *the great Farnese Palace:* The Palazzo Farnese in Rome, designed by Italian architect Antonio da Sangallo the Younger (1484–1546) with subsequent work by Michelangelo, is an imposing High Renaissance palace, now housing the French Embassy.

24 *Poughkeepsie:* A small city on the Hudson River north of New York City.

Tarantula, or, The Dance of Death

26 *Half Europe died:* The outbreak of bubonic plague—a pandemic known as the Black Death—is estimated to have killed 30 to 60 percent of Europe's population from 1348 to 1350. AH wrote, in a letter: "The symptoms of the plague were 'dance-like' convulsions resembling those brought on by the bite of a tarantula, from which the tarantella derives."

The End of the Weekend

27 *Captain Marryat:* English novelist Captain Frederick Marryat (1792–1848) was famous for his books about life at sea.

Message from the City

29 *your house, built upon sand:* Matthew 7:24–27.

Behold the Lilies of the Field

30 *Behold the Lilies of the Field:* Matthew 6:25–30. AH is using the Tyndale translation of the Bible (1526) instead of—as was his custom—the King James Version (1611).

30 *the emperor:* Publius Licinius Valerianus (c.200–260), known as Valerian in English, was Roman emperor from 253 to 260. Defeated by Persian forces at the Battle of Edessa in 260, he was taken captive by their king, Shapur I, and later killed. In his *The History of the Decline and Fall of the Roman Empire* (1766–88), Edward Gibbon wrote: "The voice of history, which is often little more than the organ of hatred or flattery, reproaches Sapor with a proud abuse of the rights of conquest. We are told that Valerian, in chains, but invested with the Imperial purple, was exposed to the multitude, a constant spectacle of fallen greatness; and that whenever the Persian monarch mounted on horseback, he placed his foot on the neck of a Roman emperor. Notwithstanding all the remonstrances of his allies, who repeatedly advised him to remember the vicissitudes of fortune, to dread the returning power of Rome, and to make his illustrious captive the pledge of peace, not the object of insult, Sapor still remained inflexible. When Valerian sunk under the weight of shame and grief, his skin, stuffed with straw, and formed into the likeness of a human figure, was preserved for ages in the most celebrated temple of Persia; a more real monument of triumph, than the fancied trophies of brass and marble so often erected by Roman vanity."

The Dover Bitch

33 *Matthew Arnold:* English poet and critic (1822–88), whose poem "Dover Beach," a meditation on moral and religious doubt, was published in 1867.

33 Nuit d'Amour: French, "Night of Love."

Three Prompters from the Wings

34 *Atropos:* In Greek mythology, the Three Fates were the goddesses of human destiny. They were sisters. Atropos, the eldest, cut the thread of mortal life with her shears. Clotho had spun the thread, and Lachesis had measured it. In this poem, the life is that of Oedipus, king of Thebes.

The Vow

42 *The mirth of tabrets:* Isaiah 24:8. Tabrets are ancient musical instruments similar to modern tambourines.

42 *The gates of horn:* To the ancients, the gates of horn and ivory are the portals through which dreams enter, the true and the false.

42 *best of all the fates:* Cf. "Chorus from *Oedipus at Colonos*," p. 160.

Rites and Ceremonies

44 *Adonoi:* Adonai, Hebrew name for God.

44 *Pleaides:* A cluster of seven stars, known as the Seven Sisters, in the constellation Taurus.

44 *treasuries of the snow:* Job 38:22.

44 *veins, brain, bones:* Cf. "The Wreck of the Deutschland" by English poet Gerard Manley Hopkins (1844–89), first stanza.

44 *lauds and threnes:* I.e., songs of praise and lamentation.

44 *Emmanuel:* Hebrew term for Messiah, literally "God with us" (cf. Matthew 1:23), a phrase that in German is *"Gott mit uns,"* itself the motto of the German military from the time of the German Empire and notably worn on the belt buckles of the Wehrmacht soldiers during World War II.

44 *An Iron Cross:* German military decoration.

45 And some there be: Ecclesiasticus 44:9.

45 *"The Singing Horses of Buchenwald":* The term used by Nazi SS officers at the Buchenwald concentration camp in World War II for Jewish prisoners chained to carts that transported heavy stones from the nearby quarry. While they worked, they were forced by guards to sing.

45 *the Pope:* Pius XII, who reigned from 1939 to 1958, has been accused of silence in the face of the Holocaust.

45 Die Vögelein: German, "The little birds fall silent in the woods," a line from the 1780 lyric "Wanderer's Night Song II" by German poet Johann Wolfgang von

Goethe (1749–1832). The forest described in Goethe's poem is where the Buchenwald concentration camp was built.

45 *the little children were suffered:* Mark 10:14.

45 "I cried unto the Lord God . . .": Psalms 3:4.

46 *The Fire Sermon:* A discourse by the Buddha about the alleviation of suffering through detachment from the senses. Also the title of the third part of *The Waste Land* by American-born English poet T. S. Eliot (1888–1965).

46 *the king of Tharsis:* A story told by Henry Knighton (d. c.1396) in his chronicles of fourteenth-century life. The Black Death, having originated in the East, swept through Europe from 1348 to 1350.

47 *Erwin von Steinbach:* German architect (c.1244–1318) whose most famous work is the Notre-Dame Cathedral in Strasbourg.

48 *And man is born to sorrow . . . :* Job 5:7.

48 *O that thou shouldst give dust . . . :* From "Denial" by English poet George Herbert (1593–1633).

49 *And let my cry come . . . :* Psalms 102:1.

49 *the Corso:* Since ancient times, Via del Corso has been a prominent street in Rome.

49 *Du Bellay:* Joachim du Bellay (c.1525–60), French poet who lived in Rome from 1553 to 1557. His sonnet "Heureux qui, comme Ulysse, a fait un beau voyage" ("Happy the man who, like Ulysses, has made a fine voyage") contrasts the magnificence of Rome with the humble pleasures of his native Anjou. Hecht's version of this poem (the French title is retained) is in *The Hard Hours.*

50 dolces: Anglicized version of *dolci,* the Italian word for sweets.

50 *Christ's Vicar:* I.e., the Pope.

50 "If I forget thee . . .": Psalms 137:5.

51 *Piranesian:* I.e., similar to the etchings of Roman ruins and imaginary prisons by the Italian artist Giovanni Battista Piranesi (1720–78), whose studio was on the Via del Corso in Rome.

51 *Yet I have seen the wicked . . . :* Psalms 37:35.

51 *Except the Lord of hosts:* Isaiah 1:9.

52 *"None does offend . . .":* Shakespeare, *King Lear,* IV.v.168.

52 *The work of thy fingers:* Psalms 8:3.

52 *The soul is thine:* This stanza uses lines from the Jewish liturgy for Yom Kippur.

52 *O deal with us according to thy name:* Cf. Jeremiah 14:7.

52 *O Lord, for thy name's sake:* Psalms 25:11.

52 *Who / Fathered the fathering rain:* Job 38:28.

53 *Forgiven be the whole Congregation:* From a prayer for Gentiles that is part of the Kol Nidre service on Yom Kippur.

53 *the promised third:* Zechariah 13:8.

53 *a nail in thy holy place:* Ezra 9:8.

53 *Neither shall the flame . . . :* Isaiah 43:2.

53 "He shall come down . . .": Psalms 72:6.

The Seven Deadly Sins

56 *Thou shalt not toil nor spin:* Matthew 6:28.

57 *"Dies Irae":* Latin, "Day of Wrath," a medieval Latin poem describing the day of judgment.

58 *Plucked out:* Matthew 5:29.

58 *Consider the ant's ways:* Proverbs 6:6.

59 *the needle's eye:* Matthew 19:24; Mark 10:25; Luke 18:25.

60 *Their savior wouldn't turn stones:* Matthew 4:3-4.

"More Light! More Light!"

62 *"More Light! More Light!":* AH wrote in a letter: "Words attributed to Goethe on his deathbed. The shrine to Goethe is at Weimar, near [the site of the] Buchenwald [concentration camp]. The first part of the poem is a composite of details of the deaths of several Renaissance martyrs, [Hugh] Latimer [c.1485–1555] & [Nicholas] Ridley [1500–1555] among them [as recounted in *Foxe's Book of Martyrs*]. The episode in the concentration camp is taken from Eugen Kogen, *The Theory and Practice of Hell*, published in 1950 by Farrar, Straus and Cudahy, Inc., in a translation by Heinz Norden from the German *Der SS Stat*."

62 *The sack of gunpowder:* The family of those about to be burned at the stake would sometimes bribe the executioner to place a sack of gunpowder in the victim's clothing, hoping the fire would quickly ignite it, kill the bound man, and spare him further suffering.

62 *Luger:* A type of pistol, invented in Germany.

"It Out-Herods Herod. Pray You, Avoid It."

64 *"It Out-Herods Herod . . .":* Shakespeare, *Hamlet*, III.ii.14.

64 *the match-girl:* The protagonist of 1845 story "The Little Match Girl" by Danish author Hans Christian Andersen (1805–75).

64 *Their cow brings forth:* Job 21:10.

65 *Childermas:* Feast on the church calendar for December 28, commemorating Herod's slaughter of the innocents.

The Cost

69 Why, let the stricken deer: Shakespeare, *Hamlet*, III.ii.277–78.

69 *Calder:* American artist Alexander Calder (1898–1976), whose most famous works are the many mobiles (a form of kinetic sculpture, consisting of hanging objects balanced on rods) he created.

69 *Trajan's column:* Monumental column, built in 113, covered with a spiral bas relief commemorating his victory over the Dacians by the Roman Emperor Marcus Ulpius Nerva Trianus, known in English as Trajan (53–117), who ruled Rome from 98 to 117. It stands in Trajan's Forum, near the Quirinal Hill in Rome.

69 *Vespa:* Italian, "wasp." A brand of Italian motor scooter.

69 *a Lapith feast:* In Greek mythology, the Lapiths were a legendary people of Thessaly. In one famous episode, they battle with and defeat centaurs who had been invited to the marriage feast of the Lapith King Pirithous but had drunkenly begun to ravish Lapith women.

70 *Gregory the Great:* St. Gregory I (c.540–604) reigned as Pope from 590 until his death.

70 *"My soul . . .":* Shakespeare, *Othello*, V.ii.1. The line is actually "It is the cause, it is the cause, my soul." Cassio, Desdemona, and Iago are also characters in the play.

70 *as Yeats would have it:* "Like a long-legged fly upon the stream / His mind moves upon silence," from the 1939 poem "Long-Legged Fly" by Irish poet William Butler Yeats (1865–1939).

Black Boy in the Dark

72 Peace, tawny slave: Shakespeare, *Titus Andronicus*, V.i.27–30.

72 *Andy Warhol:* American artist (1928–1987), pioneer of pop art.

73 *The President:* I.e., John F. Kennedy (1917–1963), assassinated in Dallas on November 22, 1963.

73 *We were there:* A reference to the line "I am the man. . . . I suffered. . . . I was there," from section 33 of the 1855 poem "Song of Myself" by American poet Walt Whitman (1819–1892).

73 *the whited sepulchres:* Matthew 23:27; Revelation 12:7–12.

Green: An Epistle

74 This urge, wrestle: From the 1948 poem "Cuttings (*later*)" by American poet Theodore Roethke (1908–63).

74 *Charlton Heston:* Hollywood actor (1923–2008).

74 *Humphrey Bogart dating Ingrid Bergman:* Actors Bogart (1899–1957) and Bergman (1915–82) are here described toward the end of the 1942 film they costarred in, *Casablanca*.

75 *darkness on the face:* Genesis 1:2.

76 *schwa:* In linguistics, the term for an indeterminate vowel usually found in a word's unstressed syllable.

76 *Brueghel's beggars:* Figures portrayed in the work of Flemish painter Pieter Brueghel the Elder (c.1525–69).

A Birthday Poem

80 *June 22, 1976:* The birthday anniversary of AH's wife, Helen.

80 *Mantegna:* Italian painter Andrea Mantegna (c.1431–1506).

80 *Holbein:* German painter Hans Holbein the Younger (c.1497–1543).

81 sub specie / Aeternitatis: Latin, from the viewpoint of eternity.

81 *Ararat:* Mount Ararat, in present-day Turkey, is said to have been where Noah's Ark landed.

81 *Zeiss:* German brand of optical instruments.

81 *Verduns and Waterloos:* Scenes of battlefield disasters. The indecisive Battle of Verdun, fought in northeastern France in 1916, left a quarter-million dead, one of the worst losses in World War I. The Battle of Waterloo, fought in Belgium in 1815, marked the end of Napoleon's rule, when he was defeated by English and Prussian forces under the Duke of Wellington and General von Blücher.

82 What is your substance: Shakespeare, Sonnet 53, ll. 1–2.

Coming Home

83 from the journals of John Clare: English poet John Clare (1793–1864), known for his accounts of rural life. Because of mental instability, worsened by the effects of depression and alcohol, he was committed to an asylum in Essex in 1837. In 1841, he left the asylum, believing that he was walking to meet his childhood sweetheart Mary Joyce, who was already three years dead. (In 1820 he had married Martha "Patty" Turner.) The poem is adapted from the "Journey Out of Essex" section of Clare's journals. Cf. *John Clare: Major Works*, ed. Eric Robinson and David Powell (Oxford: Oxford University Press, 1984), pp. 432–37.

84 a king of Babylon: I.e., Nebuchadnezzar (c.630–562 B.C.), who conquered Judea and forced the Jews into exile. The prophet Daniel relates that Nebuchadnezzar was humbled by God and made to live like a beast for seven years. Cf. Daniel 4:33.

"Auguries of Innocence"

86 *"Auguries of Innocence":* 1803 poem by English poet, artist, and visionary William Blake (1757–1827).

86 *Medean:* In Greek mythology, Medea was an enchantress who, when she discovered her husband, Jason, was unfaithful, killed his mistress and her own children.

Peripeteia

87 *Peripeteia:* Greek, "turning point." A term used in Aristotle's *Poetics* to indicate the sudden reversal of circumstances in a dramatic work.

88 *Something by Shakespeare:* I.e., *The Tempest*, whose heroine is Miranda. Her father is Prospero and her beloved is Ferdinand.

88 *Sylvia? Amelia Earhart?:* "Who is Silvia?" is a lyric from Shakespeare's *Two Gentlemen*

of Verona. American aviator Amelia Earhart (1897–1937) was the first woman to fly solo across the Atlantic Ocean, in 1928.

The Feast of Stephen

92 esprit de corps: French, "spirit of the group"; comradeship.

92 Mens sana: Latin, "a healthy mind." Part of the familiar Latin adage *mens sana in corpore sano* (a sound mind in a sound body), a line in one of the satires by the early-second-century Roman poet Juvenal.

92 pliés: French, "bends." A term in ballet for movements with bent knees and straight back.

93 Sturm-Abteilungs Kommandant: German, "assault detachment commander." The SA, called Brownshirts, were a paramilitary organization in Nazi Germany.

93 *they've got one cornered:* The story of the martyred St. Stephen, whose feast day is celebrated on December 26, is told in Acts, chaps. 6 and 7. Saul of Tarsus—after his conversion, he became St. Paul—was said (Acts 8:1) to have urged on the crowd in its frenzied execution.

The Odds

94 *My Lai:* Scene of a notorious 1968 torture and massacre by American troops of unarmed South Vietnamese civilians during the Vietnam War.

Apprehensions

96 *my brother's:* AH's brother Roger (1926–90), who went on to publish five books of poems, was from childhood afflicted with epilepsy—later in the poem referred to by its French name *"le grand mal"* ("the great disease"), which also afflicted Julius Caesar and Fyodor Dostoyevsky.

96 coups de théâtre: French, sudden dramatic turns of events.

96 *the* Journal-American: The *New York Journal American* was an afternoon newspaper published from 1937 to 1966.

97 *silence and cunning:* In the 1916 novel *A Portrait of the Artist as a Young Man* by Irish writer James Joyce (1882–1941), the hero Stephen Dedalus proclaims his artistic credo: ". . . I will try to express myself in some mode of life or art as freely as I can, and as wholly as I can, using for my defence the only arms I allow myself to use . . . silence, exile, and cunning."

97 *Roget:* Peter Mark Roget (1779–1869), British physician and lexicographer whose 1852 *Thesaurus*, a collection of related words, is a standard reference work.

97 *Arthur Rackham:* English book illustrator (1867–1939) specializing in bringing fairy tales to life with an often frightening realism.

98 *Mrs. Siddons as The Tragic Muse:* Title of a famous 1784 portrait by English painter Sir Joshua Reynolds (1723–92) of the English actress Sarah Siddons (1755–1831).

98 *Whittier . . . :* American poet John Greenleaf Whittier (1807–92); American poet Henry Wadsworth Longfellow (1807–82); "Home, Sweet Home," well-known American song written by Henry Bishop (1786–1855) and John Howard Payne (1791–1852); Dryden's remark about Geoffrey Chaucer's poetry is in the preface to his 1700 *Fables Ancient and Modern.*

98 *"The Vision of Dame Kind":* I.e., Mother Nature. From the introduction by English-American poet W. H. Auden (1907–73) to the 1964 anthology *The Protestant Mystics,* edited by Anne Fremantle.

98 *Lexington:* I.e., Lexington Avenue, on Manhattan's Upper East Side. As a child, AH lived in the Rhinelander Apartments, at 140 East 89th Street, overlooking Lexington Avenue.

100 *George Washington:* A statue of Washington stands on New York's Wall Street, on the exact spot where he was inaugurated as first president of the United States in 1789.

100 *phenobarbital:* A barbiturate used as an anticonvulsant.

100 *Cabbalistic:* Referring to the Cabbala, the body of mystical Hebrew writings.

100 *enthymemes:* Incomplete chains of reasoning.

101 *childish things:* 1 Corinthians 13:11.

101 *the Wagnerian twilight of the* Reich: The disastrous end of Hitler's vaunted thousand-year *Reich,* or rule, in 1945 likened to the destruction of the world portrayed in the 1876 opera *Götterdämmerung (The Twilight of the Gods)* by German composer Richard Wagner (1813–1883).

101 *"In der Heimat . . .":* German, "In the homeland, there we will meet again." From a German army song dating back to World War I.

The Ghost in the Martini

102 *martini with a twist:* I.e., the sliver of lemon peel flavoring the cocktail.

102 *(Aye, there's the rub.):* Hamlet, III.i.65.

102 *the famous wages / Of sin:* Romans 6:23.

103 *Apeneck Sweeney:* A caricature in the 1920 poem "Sweeney Among the Nightingales" by T. S. Eliot.

103 *Silenus:* In Greek mythology, the dissolute tutor to Dionysus, the god of wine.

103 *Samuel's ghost:* I Samuel 28:3–25.

103 *'All things shall be revealed . . .':* Matthew 10:26.

104 *'the long and the short and the tall':* From a popular British wartime song, "Bless 'Em All."

104 *'No light . . .':* Milton, *Paradise Lost,* I.62.

104 *'I have been studying . . .':* Shakespeare, *Richard II,* V.v.1–2.

"Gladness of the Best"

106 *"Gladness of the Best":* George Herbert's sonnet "Prayer," l. 10.

106 Let us get up early: Song of Solomon 7:12.

106 *a Jesse's family tree:* Reference to the Tree of Jesse in Isaiah 11:1, describing the descent of the Messiah from the family of Jesse of Bethlehem. In art, the elaborating Tree of Jesse has long been a decorative motif, notably in the famous stained-glass window in Chartres Cathedral dating from 1145.

106 *"flowres delice":* Cf. "Aprill" in the 1579 poem *Shepheardes Calender* by English poet Edmund Spenser (c.1552–99).

106 *Gobelin* millefleurs: The Gobelin firm of tapestry and carpet makers, noted for their rich designs, dates back to the fifteenth century in France. *Millefleurs* (French, "thousand flowers") is a tight and brilliant pattern of bunched blossoms.

106 *tourbillions, gerbs and golden falls:* I.e., whirlwinds, spark sprays, and gold outlines of a flower's petal.

106 *Duc de Berry's* Très Riches Heures: Jean de Valois, the Duc de Berry (1340–1416), commissioned the creation of illuminated manuscripts, the most gloriously decorated of which is a devotional book of hours, "The Very Rich Hours," made around 1410.

106 cantus: Cantus firmus is the plainsong melody that serves as the basis for a polyphonic composition.

107 *St. George:* I.e., English poet and priest George Herbert (1593–1633), who from 1630 served as rector of St. Andrew Bemerton, near Salisbury.

107 *"Domestic servant . . .":* George Herbert's response to a dubious friend's question as to why someone of Herbert's aristocratic lineage would take holy orders: "It hath been formerly judged that the domestic servants of the King of Heaven should be of the noblest families on earth," as recounted in the 1670 *The Life of Mr. George Herbert* by English writer Izaak Walton (1593–1683).

107 Riposta *for* Proposta: In a musical canon, the first melody (known as the *proposta*) is met with an imitative second melody (the *riposta*).

107 *"and with thy spirit":* In the Roman Catholic liturgy, a responsive dialogue between priest and congregation known as the Sursum Corda includes one exchange, *Dominus vobiscum* (The Lord be with you) and *Et cum spiritu tuo* (And with thy spirit).

107 *as his who claimed:* The concluding lines of George Herbert's "The Posie" (and widely recognized as his motto): "*Lesse then the least / Of all Gods mercies,* is my posie still." Cf. Genesis 32:10 and Ephesians 3:8.

The Grapes

111 *the* Hôtel de l'Univers et Déjeuner: French, "Hotel of the Universe and Lunch."

111 *the* Beau Rivage: Another hotel, meaning "The Beautiful Shore."

112 *Marlon Brando:* American actor (1924–2004) who in 1954 won an Oscar for his starring performance in the film *On the Waterfront.*

112 *Roger Bannister:* English athlete (b. 1929), and first, in 1954, to run the mile in under four minutes.

114 *The Deodand:* "Deodand is defined as 'A thing forfeited or to be given to God; *spec.* in *Eng. Law,* a personal chattel which, having been the immediate occasion of the death of a human being, was given to God as an expiatory offering, i.e., forfeited to the Crown to be applied to pious uses. . . .' The poem is based on a painting by Pierre-Auguste Renoir, called *Parisians Dressed in Algerian Costume,* in the National Museum of Western Art, Tokyo." [AH's note.]

114 *What are these women up to?:* Cf. Isaiah 3:16–26.

114 femme-de-chambre: French, "chambermaid."

114 arrondissement: French, one of the municipal districts Paris is divided into.

114 haute-bourgeoisie: French, "upper middle class."

114 tableau vivant: French, a staged scene of motionless and silent actors as if in a picture.

114 *Ingres or Delacroix:* Two great French painters, the neoclassical Jean-Auguste-Dominique Ingres (1780–1867) and the romantic Eugène Delacroix (1798–1863).

115 poissons d'or: French, "goldfish."

115 *the once queen:* Marie-Antoinette (1755–1793), queen of Louis XVI, guillotined a few months after her husband's execution in 1793.

115 *Those who will not be taught:* Cf. George Santayana, *The Life of Reason* (1906): "Those who cannot remember the past are condemned to repeat it."

115 *Racine:* French playwright Jean Racine (1639–99).

115 *the Algerian war:* Conflict between France and its colony Algeria between 1954 and 1962, resulting in Algerian independence.

116 "Donnez moi . . .": "The concluding lines in French may be rendered:

> *Let me be given nourishment at your hands*
> *Since it's for you I perform my little dance*
> *For I am the street-walker, Magdalen,*
> *And come the dawn I'll be on my way again,*
> *The beauty queen, Miss France."* [AH's note.]

The Short End

117 Here the anthem doth commence: From Shakespeare's poem "The Phoenix and the Turtle," first published in 1601.

117 *Jacobin . . . Biedermeier:* Design styles, the first named for radicals during the French Revolution, the latter for early- to mid-nineteenth-century German design modelled on the French Regency mode.

117 *Trylon and Perisphere:* Two huge modernist geometrical structures built for the 1939 New York World's Fair.

118 *The Mellon and the Berenson:* Two American art connoisseurs, banker Andrew Mellon (1855–1937) and art historian Bernard Berenson (1865–1959).

119 thé dansant: French, "tea dance."

119 *Kern, Romberg, Friml:* Three American composers of popular songs and entertainments: Jerome Kern (1885–1945), Hungarian-born Sigmund Romberg (1887–1951), and Czech-born Rudolf Friml (1879–1972).

120 *Such was this place, a hapless rural seat:* "Cf. *Paradise Lost*, Bk. IV, ll. 246–7." [AH's note.]

123 *a soft radio soundtrack:* The song is "Hello, My Baby," written by Joseph Howard and Ida Emerson, published in 1899.

125 *Stygian:* I.e., like the desolate River Styx, which in Greek mythology formed the border between earth and the underworld.

126 *the wise virgins:* Matthew 25:1–13.

126 *Which also happens to be the word for 'bitter':* "Strictly speaking it is the adverbial 'bitterly,' but this lapse is to be explained by the imperfect memory of a former student in an hour of stress." [AH's note.]

126 *Mel Tormé:* American singer (1925–1999).

126 *Kid Ory:* American trombonist and bandleader Edward "Kid" Ory (1886–1973).

126 *Stanford White:* American architect (1853–1906). Washington Square, in Manhattan's Greenwich Village, marks the southern end of Fifth Avenue.

127 *In Élysée prospectus:* I.e., in the grand dimensions and perspectives of the Champs-Élysées, the tree-lined thoroughfare in Paris.

127 *the Metropolitan's facade:* I.e., the Metropolitan Museum of Art, at Fifth Avenue and 82nd Street in New York City.

128 redivivus: Latin, "brought back to life."

128 *Shiva:* "Hindu god of destruction, associated with dancing and with fire." [AH's note.]

128 *Sardanapalus:* According to legend, the sybaritic king of ancient Assyria. It was said that, his city under siege by enemies, he gathered his wives and treasure in his palace and burned them, together with himself.

Still Life

129 *Tennysonian:* I.e., in the melancholy manner of English poet Alfred Lord Tennyson (1809–1892).

129 *Steuben glass:* American firm founded in 1903 that manufactures blown-glass forms that are subsequently engraved.

129 *Garand rifle:* The M1 semi-automatic rifle, standard for the United States armed forces in World War II.

Persistences

130 *T'ang:* Chinese dynasty from 618 to 907.

131 *REM:* "Rapid Eye Movement—a psychological indicator that a sleeper is dreaming." [AH's note.]

131 *Blue numeral tattoos:* The underside of forearms of Jews sent to Nazi concentration camps were tattooed with identification numbers.

The Venetian Vespers

134 *Burn in their slow, invisible decay:* Cf. the last line of "The Wood-Pile" by American poet Robert Frost (1874–1963).

135 *San Pantaleone:* St. Pantaleon, born in Asia Minor, was a Christian martyr who died around 305. He was venerated as the patron of physicians and midwives. His name in Greek means "the all-compassionate," but AH may here be conflating it with the Italian word *pantalone* or pants, and making thereby a farcical figure as if from the old *commedia dell'arte*.

135 Commedia: The Italian comedy of the sixteenth and seventeenth centuries, using improvisation around stock characters and situations. AH is here also playing on the great 1321 visionary poem, *La Divina Commedia* (*The Divine Comedy*) by Italian poet Dante Alighieri (1265–1321).

136 *Keystone Kops:* A series of silent film comedies, made between 1912 and 1917, about a group of hapless policemen.

136 *the fall of mercy:* See Shakespeare, *The Merchant of Venice*, IV.i.184-187; Matthew 5:45.

136 *Monet and Debussy:* French impressionist artists, painter Claude Monet (1840–1926) and composer Claude Debussy (1862–1918).

137 *Piranesian* Carceri: Cf. note to p. 50. Here Piranesi's engravings of prisons (in Italian, *carceri*) are specified.

137 acqua minerale: Italian, "mineral water."

137 *Bromo-Seltzer:* An antacid taken to relieve indigestion. It is sold in a blue bottle, the shade of which is here said to resemble an ink marketed by the French (originally American) fountain-pen manufacturers Waterman.

137 *the glory holes / Of the Murano furnaces:* Murano is an island town slightly north of Venice, famed for its glassmaking.

137 *Monte Cristos:* In the 1844 novel *Le Comte de Monte-Cristo* (*The Count of Monte Cristo*) by French novelist Alexandre Dumas (1802–70), the hero is imprisoned for fourteen years before he escapes and revenges himself.

138 *Wagner died here:* German composer Richard Wagner, who died in Venice in 1883; Russian-born American composer Igor Stravinsky (1882–1971); Italian composer Domenico Cimarosa (1749–1801).

138 *Of Byron writing:* " 'I should, many a good day, have blown my brains out, but for the recollection that it would have given pleasure to my mother-in-law . . .' From a letter to Tom Moore, January 28, 1817." [AH's note.]

138 *Thus virtues, it is said:* Cf. "Gerontion" by T. S. Eliot, ll. 46–47.

138 ménage: French, people living together.

138 *Corbaccios and corvinos,* spintriae: The first two words are related to those in Italian for ravens and carrion crows, but are here meant to imply thuggish and raven-

haired lads. Corbaccio and Corvino are scheming characters in the 1606 satiric comedy *Volpone* by English playwright and poet Ben Jonson (c.1572–1637). The final word is a plural Latin term, feminine in form, for male prostitutes.

138 Incurabili: I.e., Ospedale degli Incurabili, the Hospital for Incurables in Venice.

138 *Charon:* In Greek mythology, the ferryman of souls across the River Styx to Hades. The Calle dei Morti, or Lane of the Dead, is a Venetian street.

139 *Anubis-executioner:* In Egyptian mythology, the jackal-headed god associated with the afterlife.

139 *Byron confessed to:* " 'But I feel something, which makes me think that if I ever reach near to old age, like Swift, I shall die at "top" first.' From a diary of 1821. Once, pointing at a lightning-blasted oak, Swift [Jonathan Swift (1667–1745), Irish-born English satirist and poet] had said to Edward Young [English poet (1683–1765)], about his apprehensions of approaching madness, 'I shall be like that tree. I shall die first at the top.' " [AH's note.]

139 *Henry Fuseli:* "Johann Heinrich Füssli, later known as John Henry Fuseli, born in Zurich, February 6, 1741, died in London, April 1, 1825. Ordained a Zwinglian minister in 1761, but abandoned the ministry, first for literature and later for painting. Settled in London in 1779, where he was elected to the Royal Academy in 1790. He was a friend of Blake [William Blake (1757–1827), English poet and artist], and *The Nightmare* is probably is his best-known painting." [AH's note.]

140 *Florian's:* Caffè Florian, a popular café on the Piazza San Marco in Venice, has been in operation since 1720.

140 *Palladio's church . . . the great church of Health:* San Giorgio Maggiore, a basilica designed by Italian architect Andrea Palladio (1508–80), and Santa Maria della Salute, erected in thanksgiving for the city's deliverance from the plague in 1630.

140 Ils se promènent . . . *the* Bois: French, "they stroll." The Bois de Boulogne is a large park in Paris.

141 *this Sea of Hadria:* I.e., the Adriatic Sea.

143 *Gabrieli's horns:* Italian composer Giovanni Gabrieli (c.1554–1612) wrote music with striking sonorities specifically for St. Mark's Cathedral.

143 *Carpaccio's prostitutes:* Italian painter Vittore Carpaccio (c.1455–c.1525), whose 1490 painting *Two Venetian Ladies* now hangs in Venice's Museo Correr.

144 *the Miller of Dee:*

> *"There was a jolly miller once,*
> *Lived on the river Dee;*
> *He worked and sang from morn till night,*
> *No lark more blithe than he.*

> *And this the burden of his song*
> *Forever used to be—*

> *I care for nobody, no, not I,*
> *And nobody cares for me."* [AH's note.]

"The Miller of Dee" is a traditional folk song from the northwest of England. The last line is actually "If nobody cares for me."

144 *Emily Post:* Many editions of *Etiquette,* a guide to proper behavior in society, by American writer Emily Post (1872–1960), appeared after its first publication in 1922.

145 *three Elijahs:* According to Jewish custom, an extra place is set at the Passover table for Elijah, whose return would usher in a new messianic age. Cf. Malachai 4:5. Cf., "The Book of Yolek," the last two lines, p. 190.

145 Corpus Juris: Latin, "the body of law." A term for a compendium of laws and their interpretations.

145 *Caslon capitals:* A serif typeface designed by English designer William Caslon (1692–1766).

145 *"The Great / Atlantic & Pacific Tea Co.":* Originally a tea company founded in 1859, it grew into the large supermarket chain known as the A&P.

146 *SALADA:* A brand of tea, whose name first reminds the speaker of Saladin (c.1137–93), the chivalrous sultan of Egypt and Syria who captured Jerusalem and defended it during the Third Crusade (1189–92), and then Aladdin, the boy in the *Arabian Nights* who can summon jinns from a magic lamp and a magic ring.

146 *Carlyle . . . Mill:* Scottish author Thomas Carlyle (1795–1881) published a defense of the "dignity of labour" in his 1843 *Past and Present.* English philosopher John Stuart Mill (1806–73) published his treatise on social good and the difference between happiness and pleasure as *Utilitarianism* (1861).

148 Let Us Be Gay: A 1930 film, directed by Robert Z. Leonard. This romantic comedy starred Norma Shearer and Marie Dressler.

148 *Allagashes:* The long, scenic Allagash River is in Maine.

148 son et lumière: French, "sound and light." A nighttime theatrical entertainment usually involving music and lighting to celebrate the site.

149 *the gospel's word:* Matthew 6:34.

149 *Bull's Eye Glass:* Thick, circular, hand-blown glass used as panes in old ships and colonial homes.

150 "And the eyes of them both . . .": Genesis 3:7.

150 "I saw 't not . . .": Shakespeare, *Othello,* III.iii.339.

151 *the vision of Isaiah:* Isaiah 6.

153 *Turner's visions:* English painter J. M. W. Turner (1775–1851). His fellow painter John Constable (1776–1837) said of Turner, "He seems to paint with tinted steam, so evanescent and so airy."

153 *The fathers (and their brothers):* Jeremiah 31:29.

153 Ho fatto un fiasco: Italian, "I have made a flask." This phrase, used by glassblow-

ers when they have completed a bottle, plays on the English usage of *fiasco* as complete failure.

154 *As through those gutters of which Swift once wrote:* " 'A Description of a City Shower,' Oct. 1710." [AH's note.]

154 *Paregoric:* A medication, based on powdered opium, for antidiarrheal and analgesic uses; here used as an imagined epithet for the Virgin Mary.

154 *Silurian epochs:* The Silurian Period is an age of geologic time in the third Paleozoic Age.

154 *they shall inherit:* Matthew 5:5.

154 *as the sands of the sea:* Genesis 22:16–18.

155 *they dwell and thrive:* Acts 17:28.

155 ancien régime: French, "old order." A term used to describe the social and political system prevailing before the French Revolution in 1789.

155 *"a little more than kin":* Shakespeare, *Hamlet*, I.ii.65.

155 *I lift up mine eyes:* Psalms 121:1.

155 *Tiepolo:* Venetian painter Giovanni Battista Tiepolo (1696–1770).

156 *the death of virtuous men:* Cf. English poet and Anglican priest John Donne (1572–1631), "A Valediction: Forbidding Mourning."

156 *As though I could be saved:* Cf. *Waiting for God* by French philosopher Simone Weil (1909–43): "One of the principal truths of Christianity, a truth that goes almost unrecognized today, is that looking is what saves us." See also John Ruskin, *Modern Painters*: "The greatest thing a human soul ever does in this world is to *see* something, and tell what he saw in a plain way. Hundreds of people can talk for one who can think, but thousands can think for one who can see. To see clearly is poetry, prophecy, and religion—all in one."

156 *a wise child:* "It is a wise child that knows its own father," traditional proverb, played on by Shakespeare, *The Merchant of Venice*, II.ii.73–74.

Curriculum Vitae

159 *Banquo's:* The ghost of Banquo appears at the banquet in Shakespeare's *Macbeth*, III.iv.

Chorus from Oedipus at Colonos

160 *Chorus from* Oedipus at Colonos: A translation of the choral interlude between scenes v and vi of *Oedipus at Colonos*, the last play by the great Greek dramatist Sophocles (c.496–406 B.C.), written when he was ninety years old.

Terms

161 *Rembrandt's pain:* Dutch painter Rembrandt van Rijn (1606–1669).

162 *"Until he close . . .":* Variously attributed to authors in the ancient world, notably Herodotus and Sophocles.

Devotions of a Painter

163 *the foot-bridge:* A motif in the paintings of French impressionist Claude Monet, to whom (along with English painter John Constable) this poem may be read as a tribute.

163 *the corrupted treasures:* Matthew 6:19–20.

163 *anaglyphs:* Ornamental details carved in low relief.

Destinations

164 The harvest is past: Jeremiah 8:20.

164 *the balm of Gilead:* Jeremiah 8:22.

Meditation

166 Quattrocento put in paint: From the 1939 poem "Under Ben Bulben" by William Butler Yeats.

166 *a Brahms quintet:* German composer Johannes Brahms (1833–1897).

167 *a sacred conversation:* A motif in art (in Italian, the *sacra conversazione*) wherein the Holy Family is represented. In this case—a composite painting invented by AH— also with Sts. John the Baptist, Sebastian, Jerome, and Francis.

167 antico verde: Italian, "antique green." A type of marble flooring.

See Naples and Die

170 *It is almost time for lunch:* From the 1944 poem "Esthetique du Mal" by American poet Wallace Stevens (1879–1955). The poem opens, "He was at Naples writing letters home," and the line is actually "It was almost time for lunch."

170 padrone: Italian, "proprietor."

171 *Diana . . . Venus:* Diana, in Roman mythology, was goddess of the hunt. The goddess of love, Venus, is here described as having shapely buttocks (callipygian).

171 *Dante says: Inferno,* V, 121–22.

171 *a seventeenth-century diarist:* English writer John Evelyn (1620–1706), who kept an extensive diary of his era. The entry for February 6, 1645, describes the prostitutes of Venice.

172 *Baedeker:* The name of a popular series of travel guides.

172 niente: Italian, "nothing."

173 *Ercole:* I.e., Hercules.

174 bella figura: Italian, "good figure"—i.e., cutting a good figure or making a fine impression in the world.

175 *Bellini's painting:* Venetian painter Giovanni Bellini (c.1430–1516). His *Transfiguration of Christ,* painted about 1487, hangs in Naples' Museo Nazionale di Capodimonte.

176 pompe / Funebri: Italian, "funeral regalia."

176 balcon: French, "balcony."

176 *Capri and Procida:* Islands off the coast of Naples.

176 *the* Wandering Isles: Cf. *The Faerie Queene*, II, xii, by the English poet Edmund Spenser (c.1552–99).

177 *Grand-Guignol sections:* I.e., the theatrically horrifying accounts of Roman Emperor Tiberius Claudius Nero (42 B.C.–37 A.D.), who had a villa on Capri, as recounted in *Lives of the Caesars* by the second-century-A.D. Roman historian Suetonius.

177 *Gustave Doré:* French artist (1832–83) who illustrated an edition of Dante's *Divine Comedy* with a series of dazzling engravings.

177 *Bosch's* Temptation: Netherlandish painter Hieronymus Bosch (c.1450–1516), whose work often features grotesque figures.

179 *the surrounding countryside:* The excursion is to the area around Pozzuoli, just north of Naples, where the poet Virgil is buried.

179 Mare Morto: Italian, "Dead Sea."

179 *Sibyl's Cave:* The Sibyl of Cumae was the prophetess and priestess presiding over the Apollonian oracle. The tunnel called her "cave" was discovered in 1932, based on descriptions in Virgil's *Aeneid*, VI. Lucius Tarquinius Superbus was a legendary king of ancient Rome.

179 Grotta del Cane: Reputedly the entrance to the underworld, and so named because dogs were sent in first to gauge the noxious gases emanating from the cave.

180 wo die Zitronen blühn: German, "where the lemon trees blossom," a phrase from the the lyric "Kennst du das Land" ("Do You Know the Land"), known in English as "Mignon's Song," included in the 1796 novel *Wilhelm Meisters Lehrjahre* (*Wilhelm Meister's Apprenticeship*) by Johann Wolfgang Goethe.

180 *Dis:* An ancient Roman term for the underworld.

180 *"Whose ancient door . . .":* Cf. *Aeneid*, VI.187–88.

180 *"The way down . . .":* *Aeneid*, VI.125.

181 *Virgil had made it seem:* In the *Aeneid*, VI.638ff.

183 *the Younger Pliny:* Roman author Gaius Plinius Caecilius Secundus (61–c.112), nephew of the naturalist Pliny the Elder (Gaius Plinius Secundus, 23–79, author of the *Naturalis Historia*), who died during the eruption of Mount Vesuvius at Naples in 79 A.D.

Crows in Winter

184 *Seas of Tranquillity:* The Sea of Tranquility (in Latin, the Mare Tranquillitatis) is a large basin on the surface of the moon's northern hemisphere.

184 Cras: Latin, "tomorrow."

The Transparent Man

185 *phenol:* Carbolic acid, used as an antiseptic.

186 *Kepler:* German mathematician and astronomer Johannes Kepler (1571–1630).

The Book of Yolek

189 *The Book of Yolek:* The poem derives from "Yanosz Korczak's Last Walk" by Hanna Mortkowicz-Olczakowa, in *Anthology of Holocaust Literature*, ed. Jacob Glatstein, Israel Knox, and Samuel Margoshes (Philadelphia: Jewish Publication Society of America, 1969). The account begins: "The day was Wednesday, 5th August, 1942, in the morning."

189 Wir haben ein Gesetz: John 19:7, in Martin Luther's translation.

Death the Archbishop

195 . . . and the almond tree: Ecclesiastes 12:5.

Death the Poet

197 Et nunc in pulvere dormio: "(And now I sleep in the dust) . . . appropriated from a refrain in John Skelton's [English poet, c.1460–1529] 'Lament for the Death of the Noble Prince Edward the Fourth,' which, in turn, was borrowed from an anonymous Middle English lyric that begins, 'I hadde richesse, I hadde my helthe. . . .' " [AH's note.] Also behind this poem is the example of the "Lament for the Makars" by Scottish poet William Dunbar (c.1460–c.1520), with its Latin refrain *Timor mortis conturbat me* ("Fear of death troubles me").

197 *Grub Street:* In eighteenth-century London, a street where disreputable publishers and hack writers worked, and now a pejorative term for hasty-writing-for-little-money.

Death the Painter

199 *The powers of Joshua:* Joshua 10:12-13.

199 *Gotham:* Nickname for New York City.

199 *A poor forked animal:* Shakespeare, *King Lear*, III.iv.107.

Death the Whore

203 *glossy pages of* Victoria's Secret: I.e., the catalogue for the line of women's lingerie and other clothing.

203 *Leporello's list:* In his so-called Catalogue Aria, "Madamina, il catalogo è questo" ("My dear lady, here is the list"), Don Giovanni's servant Leporello reveals the extent of his master's sexual conquests, in Mozart's 1787 opera *Don Giovanni*.

204 *"Let the day perish . . . ":* Job 3:3.

Death the Film Director

207 *Pierrot-white:* Pierrot is a sad clown dressed in a white tunic, a stock character in French *commedia dell'arte*.

207 *Henry Mancini:* American composer of film and television music (1924–94).

207 *C.B.:* American film director Cecil B. DeMille (1881–1959), known for the extravagant style and scale of his movies.

Death the Carnival Barker

209 con brio: Italian, "with vigor"; a musical direction.

209 *Give me your poor:* " 'Give me your tired, your poor, / Your huddled masses yearning to breathe free . . . ,' " says the Statue of Liberty in the 1883 poem "The New Colossus" by American poet Emma Lazarus (1849–87), which is engraved on the statue's pedestal.

The Whirligig of Time

210 *The Whirligig of Time:* A free translation of the twenty-fifth poem ("Parcius iunctas quatiunt fenestras") in the first book of odes by Roman poet Quintus Horatius Flaccus (65 B.C.–8 B.C.), better known in English as Horace.

Là-Bas: *A Trance*

212 Là-Bas: French, "over there."

212 *Samarkand:* City in what is now Uzbekistan, but centuries earlier a fabled stop on the Silk Road, the trading route between China and the West.

212 *a Parisian poet:* I.e., Charles Baudelaire (1821–67).

212 *Houris:* Persian term for alluring women, such as those in the Koranic paradise.

212 *Carpaccio's Middle East:* Sixteenth-century Venetian painter Vittore Carpaccio, renowned as an Orientalist, often used scenes from the Middle East as background landscapes in his religious paintings.

Matisse: Blue Interior with Two Girls—1947

213 *Matisse:* French painter Henri Matisse (1869–1954). The painting now hangs in the University of Iowa Museum of Art.

213 *gnomon:* An object used to cast a shadow as indicator, as on a sundial.

214 *Once out of nature:* Cf. William Butler Yeats's poem "Sailing to Byzantium," published in 1928.

Proust on Skates

215 *Proust:* French novelist Marcel Proust (1871–1922).

215 *Engelmann's Star:* "Englemann's Star is an elaborate pattern for figure skating, devised by one E. Engelmann [Eduard Engelmann Jr.], the Austrian skating champion of Europe in 1894. The 'View of Delft' is a Vermeer [Jan Vermeer (1632–75), Dutch painter] painting that deeply impressed and affected Proust when he saw it in the Mauritshuis at The Hague in 1902." [AH's note.]

216 danseur noble: French, "noble dancer." A male ballet star who projects nobility in his style of dancing.

216 *Palmer cursives and smooth* entrelacs: The Palmer Method was a widely used method of instruction in penmanship emphasizing cursive writing. *Entrelacs* is a French term for interlaced designs.

Late Afternoon: The Onslaught of Love

221 *the caulking irons sound:* This passage is indebted to a description in the 1857 novel *Madame Bovary* by French writer Gustave Flaubert (1821–80). Cf. pt. III, chap. iii.

221 *Donatello's* David: The delicate and sensual life-sized bronze statue of the young David, made around 1430 by the Italian sculptor Donatello (c.1386–1466).

Mirror

222 Veritas: Latin, "truth." The motto of Harvard University.

222 A Mirror for Magistrates: "*A Mirror for Magistrates*, a sequence of poems by many hands concerning the theme of the Fall of Princes, of men of great authority and power, containing an *Induction*, and an account of the downfall of Henry, Duke of Buckingham, both by Thomas Sackville, Earl of Dorset [English poet, 1536–1608]." [AH's note.]

223 Ding-an-Sich: German, "thing-in-itself." A term used by German philosopher Immanuel Kant (1724–1804) to designate an object existing apart from its observer.

223 *the Daily/Mirror:* Morning tabloid newspaper published in New York from 1924 until 1963.

223 *Those shrouded regions where the meanings are:* Emily Dickinson, "There's a certain Slant of light," l. 8.

A Fall

224 *Calvin:* French theologian John Calvin (1509–64).

225 Pisse-Vache: "*Pisse-Vache* [in English, "cow piss"], mentioned by Byron in an October 8, 1816, letter to John Murray as 'one of the finest torrents in Switzerland.' " [AH's note.]

A Certain Slant

226 A Certain Slant: "The poem had its origin in a sentence in a story called 'The Boys' by Anton Chekhov [Russian playwright and story writer, 1860–1904]." [AH's note.] The poem's title alludes to the opening of a poem by American poet Emily Dickinson (1830–1886), "There's a certain slant of light, / Winter Afternoons– . . ."

226 *pavé:* French, "pavement." A method of setting small diamonds so that no metal shows.

Saul and David

227 *Saul and David:* "I Samuel 16:14–23." [AH's note.]

Judith

229 *Judith:* "Judith 10:1–23." [AH's note.]

Look Deep

230 *'the fringèd curtain':* Shakespeare, *The Tempest,* I.ii.409.

230 *a goddess:* Since this poem's subject is the iris flower, the goddess here is Iris, in Greek mythology the personification of the rainbow and messenger of the gods.

230 The Rainstorm . . . The Ring: The first is an imagined version of the Biblical Flood, and the second is the cycle of operas *Der Ring des Nibelungen* (*The Ring of the Niebelung*) by Richard Wagner, written between 1848 and 1874.

230 arc-en-ciel: French, "rainbow." See Genesis 9:13.

Sacrifice

231 *Sacrifice:* "Genesis 22:1–19." [AH's note.]

232 mach schnell . . . : German, "hurry up, get back, quite right, this minute, yessir."

233 Fahrrad!: German, "bicycle."

233 Manger?: French, "Eat?"

233 Bicyclette: French, "bicycle."

233 Nous n'avons pas de bicyclettes: French, "We have no bicycles."

The Ashen Light of Dawn

235 *The Ashen Light of Dawn:* A translation of *"Le Crépuscule du matin"* ("Morning Twilight") by Charles Baudelaire.

235 *Aurora:* In Roman mythology, the goddess of dawn.

The Road to Damascus

236 *The Road to Damascus:* "Acts 9. See also *From Jesus to Paul* by Joseph Klausner [Jewish scholar (1874–1958), whose book was published in English in 1943], pp. 325–30." [AH's note.]

236 *the falling sickness:* I.e., epilepsy.

Sarabande on Attaining the Age of Seventy-Seven

237 *Sarabande:* In the seventeenth and eighteenth centuries, a slow and stately court dance.

237 The harbingers are come: From the poem "The Forerunners" by George Herbert.

237 *withers:* The high part of the back of a horse, between its shoulder blades. Cf. Shakespeare, *Hamlet,* II.ii.252; also Thomas Hardy, "Neutral Tones."

Short Chronology

1923 Anthony Evan Hecht was born in New York City, on January 16. His father, Melvyn Hahlo Hecht (1893–1978), was a classics major at Harvard when his own father went blind and he was forced to quit school and take over his father's business, The New England Enamel Co. He later held several business posts, notably in securities, none with success. He married Dorothea Grace Holzman (1894–1979) in 1920. Both parents were descended from wealthy German Jewish families, though their money diminished with the Depression, and neither parent was observant. His younger brother, Roger (1926–1990), was also a poet, and published five books of poetry in his lifetime.

1927–40 Attended first the Dalton School (1927–1930) and then the Collegiate School in Manhattan (1930–1936), and finally the Horace Mann School for Boys in Riverdale.

1940 Entered Bard College. Although he had previously been a mediocre student (except for mathematics and geometry), during freshman year his intelligence was at last engaged, and his love of poetry flourished. Read Hopkins, Eliot, W. H. Auden, Dylan Thomas, Wallace Stevens, Hart Crane.

1942 As a nineteen-year-old junior at Bard, he signed up in the U.S. Army's Enlisted Reserve Corps in November, hoping to enter the Army Specialized Training Program.

1943 Began basic training at Fort Dix, New Jersey, then Fort McClellan, Alabama. Sent for immersion study of German to Carleton College, Northfield, Minnesota, then assigned to the 97th Infantry Division.

1944 Stationed at Fort Leonard Wood, Missouri, in the 386th Infantry Regiment, C Company, 3rd Platoon, for infantry training. July, moved to

Camp San Luis Obispo, and later Camp Callan and Camp Cooke, California, for amphibious assault training. During training he read, sometimes listlessly, sometimes voraciously—Spinoza and Marianne Moore, *Tristram Shandy* and *Finnegans Wake*, Shakespeare and Rimbaud. Because of credits earned at Carleton, AH was awarded a B.A. *in absentia* from Bard.

1945 January, the 97th Division was deployed to Le Havre, France, and in March began its move toward Germany, via Belgium and Holland. In April, the 97th Division participated in the Battle of the Ruhr Pocket, engaging in fierce firefights. On April 23, the division liberated the Flossenbürg concentration camp, an annex of Buchenwald near the Czech border, a traumatic event in Hecht's imagination and the cause of much mental anguish. He later wrote: "For years after I would wake shrieking. I must add an important point: after the war I read widely in Holocaust literature, and I can no longer separate my anger and revulsion at what I really saw from what I later came to learn." Met writer Robie Macauley, a member of the Counter Intelligence Corps. Returned to Fort Bragg, North Carolina; in August, the 97th Division was reassigned to duty in the Pacific, though Japan's surrender meant Hecht and Macauley both exchanged combat for occupation duties. Arrived in Japan in September, and reported to Kumagaya, where he worked in the Public Relations Office, writing pieces for *Pacific Stars and Stripes* and occasional scripts for broadcast on Radio Tokyo.

1946 Left Japan on February 20, and was honorably discharged from the army on March 12, at the rank of private first class. On the advice of Robie Macauley and with the help of the G.I. Bill of Rights, entered Kenyon College as a "special student," in order to study with John Crowe Ransom. Taught freshman composition.

1947 In spring, taught at Kenyon. His first poems, "Once Removed" and "To a Soldier Killed in Germany," were published in *The Kenyon Review*. In fall, served as graduate teaching assistant at the State University of Iowa, in Iowa City. Befriended Flannery O'Connor there. Following a nervous breakdown, he returned to his parents' home in New York City and entered psychoanalysis.

1947 Studied privately with Allen Tate, who recommended that AH take over Tate's teaching duties that fall at New York University. Met Robert Lowell and Jean Stafford. That summer, attended the Kenyon School of English, where he studied with William Empson, F. O. Matthiessen, and Austin Warren.

1948 His poems begin to appear in *The Hudson Review*, *Poetry*, *Furioso*. Won the *Furioso* Poetry Award. Lived with Macauley on the Lower East Side, working on an uncompleted novel. Enrolled at Columbia University as a candidate for a master's degree in English literature.

1950 Granted an M.A. by Columbia University; the title of his dissertation was "Poetry as a Form of Knowledge." Travelled to Paris; shared an apartment in Amsterdam with friend Al Millet. November, moved to Ischia, where he met W. H. Auden, who summered on the island.

1951 May, awarded the first Rome Fellowship in Literature by the American Academy of Arts and Letters, a grant allowing its recipient a year's stay at the American Academy in Rome, beginning in October. News reached AH in Ischia. Composer Lukas Foss was also in residence at the Academy, and for him AH translated selections of German poetry that became the text for a cantata, *A Parable of Death*, composed by Foss, commissioned by the Louisville Philharmonic Society; the vocal score was published by Carl Fischer in 1953.

1952–54 Instructor, Bard College. Taught freshman English, poetry writing, Renaissance poetry, and Shakespeare. Colleagues included Saul Bellow, Irma Brandeis, and Heinrich Blücher (whose wife, Hannah Arendt, also became a friend). Began to meet the poets who earned his admiration and affection throughout his life: James Merrill, Richard Wilbur, John Hollander, Richard Howard, W. S. Merwin, Anne Sexton, James Wright, W. D. Snodgrass, Howard Nemerov, Mona Van Duyn, Howard Moss, Robert Fitzgerald, Mark Strand, and William Meredith; and, some years later, Joseph Brodsky and Derek Walcott.

1954 Married Patricia Anne Harris. He later described their six-year marriage as "consistently unhappy." Given a Guggenheim Foundation fellowship. *A Summoning of Stones* published by Macmillan. Returned for a year to the American Academy in Rome, where Richard Wilbur was also in residence.

1956 Started teaching freshman English at Smith, continued until 1959, first as instructor, later as assistant professor. Colleagues included Sylvia Plath (whose husband, Ted Hughes, was also a friend), Daniel Aaron, Newton Arvin, Leonard Baskin, Helen Bacon, and Elizabeth Drew. Son Jason was born.

1958 Son Adam was born. Legal-separation document filed in August. Awarded Hudson Review fellowship.

1959 Won second Guggenheim fellowship.

1960 Awarded a Ford Foundation fellowship.

1961 In January, the divorce from Patricia Harris was finalized.

1962 Patricia Harris married Philippe Lambert in New York and moved to Brussels with the children soon after the marriage. (She and Lambert had a child, and divorced in 1973.) AH's separation from his sons caused him much anguish. In psychotherapy for depression; hospitalized for three months at Gracie Square Hospital in New York, and prescribed antidepressants.

1961–67 Teaching at Bard, first as an associate professor and then as a professor.

1965 Presented with the Brandeis University Creative Arts Award.

1966 In spring, joined the editorial board of *The Hudson Review*, advising on poetry manuscripts; served until winter 1968.

1967 Began teaching at the University of Rochester in September. *The Hard Hours* published by Atheneum. His editor there, and later at Knopf, Harry Ford, became a close friend. *Jiggery-Pokery: A Compendium of Double Dactyls*, edited by AH and John Hollander, published by Atheneum. Participated in Poetry International at Queen Elizabeth Hall in London; among the other readers were Auden, John Berryman, Pablo Neruda, Allen Ginsberg, and Robert Graves. Awarded a Rockefeller Foundation fellowship, and the Lillian Fairchild Award.

1968–69 Pulitzer Prize for *The Hard Hours*; also the Russell Loines Award, presented by the National Institute of Arts and Letters, and the Miles Poetry Prize. At the American Academy in Rome again, working with Helen Bacon on a translation of Aeschylus' *Seven Against Thebes*. Read at the Spoleto Festival. Given the Honorary Fellow grant from the Academy of American Poets. Named the John H. Deane Professor of Rhetoric and Poetry at Rochester.

1970 Became a member of the National Institute of Arts and Letters. Awarded an honorary degree by Bard.

1971 In spring, appointed a chancellor of the Academy of American Poets; served until 1995. Married Helen D'Alessandro on June 12. She had been his student at Smith and later worked in publishing in New York; became an interior designer and the author of five cookbooks. AH was Visiting Hurst Professor at Washington University, St. Louis.

1972 Awarded a lectureship in American literature by the State Department, and represented the United States at an international literary conference held in São Paulo, Brazil. Son Evan Alexander born.

1973 Visiting professor, Harvard University. Spent time with Elizabeth Bishop. Translation, with Helen H. Bacon, of *Seven Against Thebes* by Aeschylus published by Oxford University Press.

1975 Elected a fellow of the American Academy of Arts and Sciences.

1977 Visiting professor, Yale University. *Millions of Strange Shadows* published by Atheneum.

1979 *The Venetian Vespers* published by Atheneum.

1981 Given the English Speaking Union Award in Poetry, and an honorary degree by Georgetown University.

1982 Charles Flint Kellogg Award in Poetry from Bard College.

1982 In August, named Consultant in Poetry to the Library of Congress. Served until 1984.

1983 Shared with John Hollander the Bollingen Prize for Poetry, given by Yale University's Beinecke Library. Awarded an honorary degree by Towson State University. Made a trustee of the American Academy in Rome.

1984 Given the Librex-Guggenheim Eugenio Montale Award for Poetry, presented on stage at the Teatro alla Scala in Milan.

1985 Named University Professor at Georgetown University and moved permanently to Washington, D.C. (Retired in 1993.)

1986 *Obbligati: Essays in Criticism* published by Atheneum.

1987 Honorary degree from the University of Rochester. *The Essential George Herbert*, edited and introduced by AH, published by Ecco Press. Given the Harriet Monroe Award by *Poetry* magazine.

1988 Awarded the Ruth B. Lilly Poetry Prize by *Poetry* magazine.

1989 Given an honorary degree by St. John Fisher College, Rochester, New York, and the Aiken-Taylor Award for Modern American Poetry by the University of the South. Grant from the National Endowment for the Arts.

1990 *The Transparent Man* and *Collected Earlier Poems* published by Knopf. Awarded a Rockfeller Foundation fellowship for a six-week residence at the Villa Serbelloni in Bellagio, Italy. Befriended novelist Edmund White, also in residence there. The classicist and translator William Arrowsmith died, ending a collaboration with AH; they had been working on a translation of Sophocles' *Oedipus at Colonus*, left uncompleted.

1992 Delivered *On the Laws of the Poetic Art*, the A. W. Mellon Lectures on the Fine Arts, at the National Gallery of Art, Washington, D.C.

1993 *The Hidden Law: The Poetry of W. H. Auden* published by Harvard University Press.

1995 *On the Laws of the Poetic Art* published by Princeton University Press.

1996 *Flight Among the Tombs* published by Knopf.

1997 First of three Bogliasco Fellowships for residence at the Centro Studi Ligure in Italy; the other stays were in 1999 and 2004. Given the Wallace Stevens Award by the Academy of American Poets and the Corrington Award by Centenary College of Lousiana.

2000 Pancreatic surgery. Awarded the Robert Frost Medal by the Poetry Society of America.

2001 *The Darkness and the Light* published by Knopf.

2002 *The Darkness and the Light* presented with the Ambassador Book Award by the English Speaking Union at the New York Public Library. Heart surgery at Cleveland Clinic.

2003 *Collected Later Poems* published by Knopf. *Melodies Unheard: Essays on the Mysteries of Poetry* published by Johns Hopkins University Press.

2004 Given the Los Angeles Times Book Prize for *Collected Later Poems*. Died of lymphoma on October 20. Buried in the cemetery at Bard College. National Medal for the Arts was awarded posthumously by President George W. Bush; in 2005, posthumously awarded an honorary degree by Ohio Wesleyan University.

Suggestions for Further Reading

By Anthony Hecht

Collected Earlier Poems. New York: Alfred A. Knopf, 1990.

Collected Later Poems. New York: Alfred A. Knopf, 2003.

Aeschylus, *Seven Against Thebes.* Translated with Helen H. Bacon. New York: Oxford University Press, 1973.

Obbligati: Essays in Criticism. New York: Atheneum, 1986.

The Hidden Law: The Poetry of W. H. Auden. Cambridge, Mass.: Harvard University Press, 1993.

On the Laws of the Poetic Art. Princeton: Princeton University Press, 1995.

Melodies Unheard: Essays on the Mysteries of Poetry. Baltimore: Johns Hopkins University Press, 2003.

About Anthony Hecht

Dowling, Gregory. "Calm Suspension," in *Someone's Road Home: Questions of Home and Exile in American Narrative Poetry.* Udine, Italy: Campanetto Editore, 2003.

German, Norman. *Anthony Hecht.* New York: Peter Lang, 1989.

Howard, Richard. "What Do We Know of Lasting Since the Fall?" In *Alone with America: Essays on the Art of Poetry in the United States Since 1950.* New York: Atheneum, 1980; enlarged ed.

Hoy, Philip. *Anthony Hecht in Conversation.* London: Between the Lines, 2004 (3rd ed.).

Lea, Sydney, ed. *The Burdens of Formality: Essays on the Poetry of Anthony Hecht.* Athens: University of Georgia Press, 1989.

Lindsay, Geoffrey. " 'Laws That Stand for Other Laws': Anthony Hecht's Dramatic Strategy." In *Essays in Literature,* vol. 21 (1994).

Oostdijk, Diederik. *The Nightmare Fighters: American Poets of World War II.* Columbus: University of South Carolina Press, 2011.

Post, Jonathan F. S. "Anthony Hecht (1923–2004): Selections from Seven Decades of Correspondence," *The Hopkins Review* (vol. 3, no. 1, Winter 2010).

———. "The Genesis of Venice in Anthony Hecht's 'Venetian Vespers,' " *The Hopkins Review* (vol. 3, no. 2, Spring 2010).

———. "Donne, Discontinuity, and the Proto-Post Modern: The Case of Anthony Hecht," *John Donne Journal* (vol. 26, 2007).

Ricks, Christopher. *True Friendship: Geoffrey Hill, Anthony Hecht, and Robert Lowell Under the Sign of Eliot and Pound.* New Haven: Yale University Press, 2010.

Spiegelman, Willard. "The Moral Imperative in Anthony Hecht, Allen Ginsberg, and Robert Lowell." In *The Didactic Muse: Scenes of Instruction in Contemporary American Poetry.* Princeton: Princeton University Press, 1989.

Index of Titles

J. D. McClatchy is the author of six volumes of poems and three collections of essays. He has also served as editor of many other volumes of poetry, including *The Vintage Book of Contemporary American Poetry* and James Merrill's *Selected Poems*. He teaches at Yale and is the editor of *The Yale Review*. He lives in Stonington, Connecticut.

A NOTE ON THE TYPE

This book was set in Baskerville, a facsimile of the type cast from the original matrices designed by John Baskerville. The original face was the forerunner of the modern group of typefaces.

Composed by Creative Graphics,
Allentown, Pennsylvania

Printed and bound by RR Donnelley,
Crawfordsville, Indiana